C. S. Lewis

My thanks to Cindy B., who first introduced
me to Lewis,
who in turned changed my life,
and now threatens to take over what I teach!

And to Rose, who helped in so many ways.
My lasting gratitude.

C. S. Lewis

A Guide to His Theology

David G. Clark

Blackwell
Publishing

© 2007 by David G. Clark

BLACKWELL PUBLISHING
350 Main Street, Malden, MA 02148–5020, USA
9600 Garsington Road, Oxford OX4 2DQ, UK
550 Swanston Street, Carlton, Victoria 3053, Australia

The right of David G. Clark to be identified as the Author of this Work has been asserted in accordance with the UK Copyright, Designs, and Patents Act 1988.

First published 2007 by Blackwell Publishing Ltd

1   2007

Library of Congress Cataloging-in-Publication Data

Clark, David George, 1943–
    C.S. Lewis : a guide to his theology / by David G. Clark.
        p. cm.
    Includes bibliographical references and index.
    ISBN 978-1-4051-5883-1 (hardcover : alk. paper)—ISBN 978-1-4051-5884-8
(pbk. : alk. paper) 1. Lewis, C. S. (Clive Staples), 1898–1963—Religion. I. Title.

BX5199.L53C53 2007
230.092—dc22

                                        2006037931

A catalogue record for this title is available from the British Library.

Set in 10/12.5pt Meridian
by SPi Publisher Services, Pondicherry, India
Printed and bound in Singapore
by Fabulous Printers Pte Ltd

The publisher's policy is to use permanent paper from mills that operate a sustainable forestry policy, and which has been manufactured from pulp processed using acid-free and elementary chlorine-free practices. Furthermore, the publisher ensures that the text paper and cover board used have met acceptable environmental accreditation standards.

For further information on
Blackwell Publishing, visit our website:
www.blackwellpublishing.com

Contents

Abbreviations

Lewis's Works

AOM   *The Abolition of Man or Reflections on Education with Special Reference to the Teaching of English in the Upper Forms of Schools*. New York: Macmillan, 1955 (1943).

BOX   *Boxen: The Imaginary World of the Young C. S. Lewis*. Walter Hooper, ed. San Diego: Harcourt Brace, 1986 (1985).

CR   *Christian Reflections*. Walter Hooper, ed. Grand Rapids: Eerdmans, 1975 (1967).

CLII   *The Collected Letters of C. S. Lewis: Books, Broadcasts, and the War 1931–1949*. Vol. II. Walter Hooper, ed. San Francisco: Harper San Francisco, 2004.

FL   *The Four Loves*. San Diego: Harcourt Brace, 1988 (1960).

GD   *The Great Divorce: A Dream*. New York: Simon & Schuster, 1996 (1946).

GID   *God in the Dock: Essays on Theology and Ethics.* Walter Hooper, ed. Grand Rapids: Eerdmans, 2001 (1979).

GO   *A Grief Observed.* By N. W. Clerk (Pseudonym). New York: Seabury Press, 1961.

HHB   *The Horse and His Boy.* Book 5. New York: Collier Books, 1977 (1954).

L   *Letters of C. S. Lewis.* Revised and Enlarged Edition. Walter Hooper, ed. San Diego: Harcourt Brace, 1993 (1966).

LAL   *Letters to an American Lady* (Mary Willis Shelburne). Clyde S. Kilby, ed. Grand Rapids: Eerdmans, 1967.

LB   *The Last Battle: A Story for Children.* Book 7. New York: Collier Books, 1977 (1956).

LTM   *Letters to Malcomb: Chiefly on Prayer.* San Diego: Harcourt Brace, 1964.

LWW   *The Lion, the Witch and the Wardrobe: A Story for Children.* Book 1. New York: Collier Books, 1977 (1950).

M   *Miracles: A Preliminary Study.* New York: Macmillan, 1965 (1947).

MC   *Mere Christianity.* New York: Macmillan, 1960 (1952).

MN   *The Magician's Nephew.* Book 6. New York: Collier Books, 1977 (1955).

OOW   *Of Other Worlds: Essays and Stories.* Walter Hooper, ed. San Diego: Harcourt Brace, 1966.

OSP   *Out of the Silent Planet.* New York: Macmillan, 1965 (1938).

P   *Poems.* Walter Hooper, ed. San Diego: Harcourt Brace, 1992 (1964).

PC   *Prince Caspian: The Return to Narnia.* Book 2. New York: Collier Books, 1977 (1951).

PER	*Perelandra*. New York: Simon & Schuster, 2003 (1943).
PP	*The Problem of Pain: How Human Suffering Raises Almost Intolerable Intellectual Problems*. New York: Macmillan, 1962 (1940).
PR	*The Pilgrim's Regress: An Allegorical Apology for Christianity, Reason and Romanticism*. Grand Rapids: Eerdmans, 1977 (1933).
ROP	*Reflections on the Psalms*. New York: Harcourt Brace, 1958.
SBJ	*Surprised by Joy: The Shape of My Early Life*. New York: Harcourt Brace, 1955.
SC	*The Silver Chair*. Book 4. New York: Collier Books, 1977 (1953).
SL&SPT	*The Screwtape Letters with Screwtape Proposes a Toast*. Revised Edition. New York: Macmillan, 1982 (1942).
SLE	*Selected Literary Essays*. Walter Hooper, ed. Cambridge: Cambridge University Press, 1980 (1969).
SMRL	*Studies in Medieval and Renaissance Literature*. Collected by Walter Hooper. Cambridge: Cambridge University Press, 1979 (1966).
THS	*That Hideous Strength*. New York: Simon & Schuster, 1996 (1945).
TWHF	*Till We Have Faces: A Myth Retold*. San Diego: Harcourt Brace, 1984 (1956).
VDT	*The Voyage of the Dawn Treader*. Book 3. New York: Collier Books, 1977 (1952).
WG	*The Weight of Glory and Other Addresses*. San Francisco: Harper Collins, Zondervan, 2001 (1949).
WLN	*The World's Last Night and Other Essays*. New York: Harcourt Brace Jovanovich, 1973 (1960).

Books of the Bible

Biblical quotations are from the New Revised Standard Version.

Gen	Genesis
Exo	Exodus
Lev	Leviticus
Num	Numbers
Deut	Deuteronomy
2 Chron	2 Chronicles
Psa	Psalms
Isa	Isaiah
Jer	Jeremiah
Ezek	Ezekiel
Dan	Daniel
Matt	Matthew
Mark	
Luke	
John	
Acts	
Rom	Romans
1 Cor	1 Corinthians
2 Cor	2 Corinthians
Eph	Ephesians
Phil	Philippians
Col	Colossians
1 Thess	1 Thessalonians
2 Thess	2 Thessalonians
1 Tim	1 Timothy
2 Tim	2 Timothy
Heb	Hebrews

James	
1 Pet	1 Peter
2 Pet	2 Peter
1 John	
Rev	Revelation

Introduction

Another book about C. S. Lewis? Well, yes, because there is still more to say. Those who have written before me have (in many cases) carefully uncovered the facts of his life and his professional accomplishments. I applaud their many contributions. Now, it's time to add to them with a comprehensive overview of his theological views. If this is your first encounter with Lewis, you'll discover just how interesting (and brilliant) he was. And if you have already read many of his books, there will still be some surprises along the way.

I mentioned that there is still more to say, so let me explain my plans for this book. By occupation, I have been a college, seminary, and university professor of New Testament and Greek for more than thirty years. But I also have an "academic hobby"; I've been privileged to teach courses on the life and thought of Lewis during that time. By "thought" I mean mostly his theology rather than his contributions to the field of English literature, since theology is my field of choice and professional contributions.

As I have discussed Lewis with my students over the years, it has become obvious to me that although Lewis was not a theologian by profession, that keen mind of his probed into just about every "corner" of the Bible, as he struggled (as all thoughtful believers do) to understand what he found there. He pondered the miracles of the Bible and the life and redemptive work of Christ. He probed into the life of the soul between death and resurrection, and speculated about the form our resurrected bodies might take. He discussed humanity in relation to animals, other humans, and even angels; both good and fallen. And this is only a partial list.

Nor were his interests only intellectual. To his credit, Lewis showed himself to be a Christian who regularly came to the Scriptures for spiritual nourishment. Douglas Gresham, Lewis's stepson, recalls Lewis faithfully reading the Bible every day. Lewis wrote that he didn't mind taking a slow train that stopped in every station because it gave him time to read and pray. Using what he learned by study and experience, he mentored others who shared his faith, giving encouragement, insights, warnings, and advice.

Finally, Lewis not only studied, believed, and lived the Scriptures, he applied what he understood to his world. Whether the subject was the history of the world, human nature, modern science, space travel, whether major or minor topics, the Bible provided the lens through which he understood everything. And so I'd like to "come alongside" Lewis to throw some light upon his insights into the Bible and their implications. Just as a knowledge of English literature is necessary to understand the "academic" Lewis, a more-than-passing familiarity with the Scriptures is also required for his many theological works. And the need for a Biblical background is particularly important because the Bible is by far the most influential source for the "religious" Lewis, and because most people today who read Lewis read the "religious" Lewis.

Lewis and Scripture

Perhaps this would be the best place for a brief autobiographical note. I've devoted my life to Biblical scholarship because I personally hold the Scriptures to be the Word of God, not the writings of Lewis. So why am I "leaving," in a sense, the divinely inspired Scriptures to study and write about the beliefs of a "mere human?" Because Lewis has helped so many (including me) better understand the Bible in such a way that his readers come away more resolved to live as Christians, no matter what the cost.

There is another reason I have taken this approach. When Lewis wrote for other Christians, he freely referred to Scriptures and often directly quoted them. But when he reached out to non-believers in books like the Ransom Trilogy or *The Chronicles of Narnia*, he was much more subtle in his use of the Bible. He knew such readers would avoid anything that was overtly theological, so why scare them away? But the Bible is still there, if disguised, and I intend to bring it out into the open.

Finally, and I need to be careful here, Lewis often went further than the Bible. By this I mean he often brings together Bible verses that speak to a subject and then, using both logic and imagination in ways that are consistent with Christian theology, develops the implications of things the Bible only hints at. For example, Paul wrote that all creation, groaning under the consequences of sin, is waiting for "the revealing of the children of God," and one day will obtain the freedom of those children (Rom 8:18–23). But does Paul believe there is a cause and effect relationship between the revealing of God's people and creation being liberated? He doesn't say, but Lewis certainly believes so, and has much to say about it. In such cases I believe I can explain the complexity of his insights, and also show how they interpret the Scriptures.

The Strengths of Lewis

Turning from the theology of Lewis to his writings in general, what strengths do his letters, poetry, articles, and books reveal? Why do his writings continue to sell in numbers that make most authors envious? Why are there more than two hundred Lewis societies that exist to discuss his works? Well, not necessarily in order of importance, here are some points that come to mind.

Lewis not only had something to say on just about any topic, he had a gift for putting his thoughts into words. He is universally praised on that score, even by those who don't agree with his views. I don't mean that everyone understands everything he said, because he frequently refers to older books that many people today haven't read. He also had a tremendous vocabulary that sends many readers to their dictionaries for help. But even those who can't follow all his references agree that he expressed himself clearly and succinctly. He even wrote to children – he was comfortable on their level, and he made them feel comfortable.

In addition to clarity, Lewis often used humor and wit when he explained his views about Christian beliefs and conduct. But they didn't cheapen his theology, and they have held the interest of many readers who wouldn't otherwise have gotten very far. When Lewis wrote *The Screwtape Letters*, humor was indispensable in helping him avoid a gloomy and depressing atmosphere as Screwtape explains the techniques of temptation and boasts of his successes in guiding his former "patients" into Hell. But throw in some humorous sounding names (Wormwood, Triptweze) and situations (Wormwood getting intoxicated because war has broken out, or Screwtape losing his cool at Wormwood's ineptitude and turning into a centipede!) and the book becomes not only bearable, but a widely enjoyed Christian classic.

Next, Lewis found room for the imagination in theology. In fact he described *The Screwtape Letters* as "ethics served with an imaginative seasoning" ("Letter to Dr. Wendell W. Watters" in L: 413, 25 October 1951). Lewis demonstrates that humor and imagination can be compatible with a reverent approach to Scripture and to one's relationship with God. In most cases, the Bible does not give structured, well-developed explanations of doctrines. Also, symbols and metaphors need to be interpreted and modern readers need help understanding ancient viewpoints from cultures that were very different from modern western cultures. The strength of Lewis is that he used his imagination to bridge different cultures and to envision how many Biblical prophecies might be fulfilled.

His imagination also helped his readers get "outside" of themselves so they could see themselves and their world from a different *perspective*. This gift of Lewis – to look at things from different sides and to help us do the same – is so important (but often overlooked by his admirers) that I need to devote a little extra space to it here in the introduction. In 1945, Lewis was invited to address a group of Anglican priests and youth leaders in Carmarthen, Wales, on the subject of apologetics. He began on a humble note, typical for him: "I'm not qualified to address people like you," and then went on to give very sound and useful advice.

The topic of perspective was a prominent theme in his advice to them. Since they were to serve the church as apologists for the faith, they would be pulled in two different directions: were they keeping up with recent developments in theology, and were they standing firm in the faith? The second, for Lewis, was far more important.

> Our upbringing and the whole atmosphere of the world we live in make it certain that our main temptation will be that of yielding to winds of doctrine, not that of ignoring them. We

are not at all likely to be hidebound: we are very likely indeed to be slaves of fashion. If one has to choose between reading the new books and reading the old, one must choose the old: not because they are necessarily better but because they contain precisely those truths of which our own age is neglectful. The standard of permanent Christianity must be kept clear in our minds and it is against that standard that we must test all contemporary thought. ("Christian Apologetics" in GID: 92)

Lewis is actually making two points here. Apologists need to keep in mind the orthodox beliefs of historical Christianity because they provide the perspective needed to judge the soundness of new expressions of doctrines and conduct. But the more general principle is that older books help us see our world through the eyes of those who saw the world much differently than we do. Lewis felt the value of older books so strongly that he wrote a separate article just to make this point.

Every age has its own outlook. It is especially good at seeing certain truths and specially liable to make certain mistakes. We all, therefore, need the books that will correct the characteristic mistakes of our own period. And that means the old books... The only palliative is to keep the clean sea breeze of the centuries blowing through our minds, and this can be done only by reading old books. Not, of course, that there is any magic about the past. People were no cleverer then than they are now; they made as many mistakes as we. But not the *same* mistakes. ("On the Reading of Old Books" in GID: 202)

Humor, imagination, and perspective all combine when Lewis writes from the point of view of Herodotus (an ancient Greek historian) trying to understand the strange Christmas customs of the foreign land of Niatirb (*Britain* spelled backward.):

And when they find cards from any to whom they also have sent cards, they throw them away and give thanks to the gods that this labour at least is over for another year. But when they find cards from any to whom they have not sent, then they beat their breasts and wail and utter curses against the sender; and, having sufficiently lamented their misfortune, they put on their boots again and go out into the fog and rain and buy a card for him also. And let this account suffice about Exmas-cards. ("Xmas and Christmas" in GID: 302)

Through Ransom's adventures on Mars (*Out of the Silent Planet*) and Venus (*Perelandra*), both unfallen planets in this fictional series, Lewis can show just how fallen earth really is. When Ransom arrives on Venus and cautiously tries one of the fruits he finds there, the taste is beyond delicious. "For one draught of this on earth wars would be fought and nations betrayed" (PER: 37). *The Screwtape Letters* provides yet another way to view humanity: from the perspective of fallen angels, or devils. Yes, Lewis really does believe that Satan and other angels, in revolt against God, have joined in common purpose through the motivations of fear and greed to frustrate God's purposes by leading as many humans as possible away from him. Lewis certainly could have written a "normal" book of practical advice for Christian living as many others have, but letting us see things from Satan's perspective is so new and effective that he has created a classic.

As Lewis examined God's creation he realized that humans have much in common with animals as well as angels. Chapter four of this book will focus upon the insights into humanity that Lewis found by looking "up" from the perspective of animals. He often used the technique of "humanizing" them to do this, and this adds to the enjoyment of his stories. After all, people all over the world bring some animals into their homes, give them names, clothes, etc. In *The Chronicles of Narnia*, Jesus himself comes in the form of a lion. The beavers help the children escape the Queen and find Aslan, and note the title of the fifth book of the series: *The Horse and His Boy*. The animals in *The Chronicles*, sad to say, often conduct themselves more wisely and kindly than do the humans.

Lewis even offered himself as a "specimen" with a valuable perspective, as chapter two will show. The educational philosophy in Britain was changing (and the same could be said about America), so that the Greek and Roman classics which, with the Scriptures, are the foundation of western civilization, were disappearing from the curriculum. The Christian faith which had influenced the values and institutions of western countries for more than a millennium was being replaced by science and technology in a post-Christian Europe. Lewis knew he was defending a losing cause.

And many other changes were occurring, and with increasing speed; changes in politics, poetry, the arts, and, of course, technology. The latter, in fact, had become so dominant in the West that now the assumption was that science, especially medicine, not Christianity, would provide the solutions to life's problems. Lewis knew that other times had also seen significant changes, such as the fall of the Roman Empire, but he argued in his inaugural Cambridge address that the changes that began around the time of 1800 were greater than any before. He concluded that address with the statement that his education placed him on the earlier side of that "great divide," making him a dinosaur (yes, he used that word); a member of a species that would soon be extinct. As a "dinosaur" Lewis put forward himself (much as an old book) as someone with a useful perspective on history; he could see the vast changes that others could not.

The ability Lewis had to "stand back" and see his world from different perspectives, often by using older books, helped him distance himself from his own times. Lewis thereby saw things in their larger context; he viewed the forest instead of individual trees. When he sought to understand his world, he stood back and surveyed the ages leading up to the twentieth century. Had he studied only his century, the unprecedented changes around him would have gone unnoticed. When he studied himself and humanity in general, as we will see in chapter four, he included the animals below us in creation and the angels above us. And once again, the larger context led to significant discoveries for the future of humanity.

Lewis expressed this variety of perspectives well because he had a great vocabulary at his command, extending even beyond the English language. In fact, he corresponded in Latin with two Italian priests. In his mother tongue, he also had a natural gift of using his vocabulary to communicate abstract concepts. Metaphors abound in his writing and the mental pictures they create greatly assist the reader. In one sense, Lewis had no choice but to use metaphorical language. Theology often treats subjects such as Heaven and Hell that are not perceived by the physical senses; yet the only language we have is the language of our physical world (MC: 74). Metaphor bridges this gap, using concrete terms to better explain abstract concepts. Lewis was a master of the skill of choosing apt and useful metaphors, and also grasping (note that "grasping" is a metaphor; one doesn't seize an idea with the hand) what Bible metaphors reveal about God.

For example, after describing how learning more and more about Norse legends did not bring him the joy he experienced from them earlier in life, he adds: "I woke from building the temple to find that the God had flown" (SBJ: 165). Or when Lewis wanted to explain how God has left his influence upon the universe, he hit upon the idea of a postman leaving packets at each house. When we open the one addressed to us, we find the moral law that seeks to direct our actions, and so we can conclude that the other packets also contain letters of instructions – for example, the law of gravity which material objects must obey (MC: 19). Such comparisons are sprinkled throughout his writings, and surely number in the hundreds.

Lewis not only could express himself well, he had a lot to say. His learning (and memory) was extensive, to say the least. He knew the important works of English literature from the inception of the English language. Philosophy was familiar territory. He studied Greek, Latin, and Scandinavian mythologies, and usually in their original languages. After his conversion, though he would be the first to say he was an amateur theologian, he made excellent progress in his study of the Scriptures, as his theological books attest. He seems to have read just about everything, and remembered almost everything he read! His autobiography (*Surprised by Joy*) recounts the first half of his life, and by then he has already read many more books than most "normal" people would ever read in a lifetime.

All of these strengths (and others that I haven't mentioned) in combination help explain the contributions that Lewis has bequeathed to his readers. He had important insights into the history of English literature, which I'll leave for others in that field to explain. He defended, with even more insights, the Christian faith. Perhaps even more importantly, he *explained* Christianity in ways that just about anyone can understand. And because he kept to the central doctrines, or "mere Christianity" as he liked to call it, Christians of many different denominations (or none at all) are able to enjoy and benefit from what he had to say.

Lewis the Apologist and Mentor

But just who did Lewis have in mind as he defended and explained? On the one hand, he wrote to reach his post-Christian readers who thought that Christianity had been tried in the past and found wanting. Not so, he argued; it's the one faith that really makes sense of this world. On the other hand, he defended the faith against those he called "liberal Christians." "They genuinely believe that writers of my sort are doing a great deal of harm" (LTM: 118).

If Christianity is to survive, they would argue, it must be demythologized, which really comes down to getting rid of the miraculous. Miracles just won't fly in a modern, scientific society that has moved past such primitive explanations of how and why things happen as they do.

> It follows that, to them, the most mischievous people in the world are those who, like myself, proclaim that Christianity essentially involves the supernatural. They are quite sure that belief in the supernatural never will, nor should, be revived, and that if we convince the world that it must choose between accepting the supernatural and abandoning all pretence of Christianity, the world will undoubtedly choose the second alternative. It will thus be we, not the liberals, who have really sold the pass. We shall have reattached to the name *Christian* a deadly scandal from which, but for us, they might have succeeded in decontaminating it. (LTM: 119)

Lewis is not the first to discover that the enemies of the gospel sometimes come from within the church itself, and like the apostles and fathers of the church before him, he took up the cause of defending the faith. To remove the supernatural, he argued, is to take away the power of the message as well, since the faith stands upon such doctrines as the creation, the incarnation, the resurrection, and the Second Coming – miraculous all. "By the way," Lewis adds, "did you ever meet, or hear of, anyone who was converted from skepticism to a "liberal" or "demythologized" Christianity? I think that when unbelievers come in at all, they come in a good deal further" (LTM: 119).

Nobody would compare Lewis to someone like Billy Graham who has invited millions to the faith, but Lewis did want to see people converted. In his own way, he was an evangelist, offering a "real" gospel that liberals could not. He pointed people to Christ with gentleness, logic, and simplicity. He knew that many of his contemporaries would never knowingly pick up a book on theology. And if they did, they wouldn't be able to understand it.

> When I began, Christianity came before the great mass of my unbelieving fellow-countrymen either in the highly emotional form offered by revivalists or in the unintelligible language of highly cultured clergymen. Most men were reached by neither. My task was therefore simply that of a *translator* – one turning Christian doctrine, or what he believed to be such, into the vernacular, into language that unscholarly people would attend to and could understand. ("Rejoinder to Dr. Pittenger" in GID: 183)

As a "translator," Lewis explained the logic of Christian doctrines in a series of radio addresses, later published as *Mere Christianity*, one of the most successful apologetic works of the twentieth century. He even was willing to visit workers in a factory during lunch time and answer their questions about religion ("Answers to Christianity" in GID: 48–62).

Lewis was also a "smuggler" of Christianity, bringing Biblical truths into his imaginative books under the guise of science fiction (*Out of the Silent Planet*, *Perelandra*, and *That Hideous Strength*). He also used the power of *story*, or myth, which has had universal appeal in all cultures at all times and places in the history of the world, in *The Chronicles of Narnia*. The first volume of *The Chronicles*, *The Lion, the Witch and the Wardrobe*, recounts the redemption work of Christ in an imaginary world, just as *Perelandra* does on the planet Venus.

Finally, Lewis not only led people to faith, including Joy Davidman Gresham, the woman who would become his wife; he mentored and encouraged them in their new walk with God. Only God knows how many people wrote him with their problems and questions, and Lewis was careful to respond to each, even while coping with a very busy schedule, many interruptions in the household, illnesses, and eventually arthritis in the fingers and other physical problems. And yet Lewis undertook even more "correspondence." In the name of Screwtape, Lewis revealed the pitfalls of the enemy each believer must face in a series of imaginary letters. To a fictional person named Malcomb, Lewis again wrote letters to instruct new believers in spiritual disciplines, particularly the prayer life.

So, taking all these ingredients into account yields the recipe known as Lewis. Take one English professor and add large amounts of history, Scripture, and literature. Stir in religious experiences and mix well. Let the mixture simmer for several decades, while serving up various portions on hundreds of paper pages. Season mixture well with wit and humor, and generously sprinkle in metaphors before serving. Let's enjoy!

Chapter 1

From Atheist to Apologist

"Lucy looks into the wardrobe for the first time."
Illustration © 2007 by Deborah Wilson Camp

I believe in Christianity as I believe that the Sun has risen, not only because I see it, but because by it I see everything else.
                                                    ("Is Theology Poetry?" in WG: 140)

Once upon a time, far out into the country, there lived an old Professor in a large house. He had no wife, but he didn't live alone. A housekeeper and three servants fixed the meals, tended the garden, and kept the cobwebs away (well, most of them). But when the war came, even more people came to live there. You see, the enemy sent up rockets that came down upon the city of London. They weren't aimed very well, but they still killed many people and scared everyone since no one knew where the next one might explode. So sensible (and brave) people did the sensible thing; they sent their children out into the country to live with kind folk who would take them in for a time.

Most professors are kind folk, and the Professor in the big house was no exception. And so, four more people came to live with the four who were already there. The names of the children were Lucy (the youngest), Edmund (next youngest), who found the Professor so funny looking when they first met he had to pretend to be blowing his nose to hide his laughter, Susan, and Peter. It wasn't long before they set off to explore their new surroundings . . . but I'm sure you already know the story about how Lucy discovered Narnia in the back of a wardrobe in one of the spare rooms.

Well, perhaps C. S. Lewis didn't live in such an enormous house, but he was a professor, his own godson did find him amusing to look at, he did live out in the country, and children did come to stay with him for their protection during World War II. One of them even remembers climbing out of a window, joining Lewis on the sly, and heading off to town together for some fish and chips when there hadn't been enough dinner!

Growing Up

Just how did a scholarly English professor with no children of his own come to write seven books for them? The explanation begins, logically enough, when he was a child himself. Both Jack (so he wished to be called) and his brother Warren found drawing pictures easier than making things since they inherited thumbs with only one joint. Warren liked cars and trains while Jack drew "dressed animals" (SBJ: 6), and their pictures soon led to stories, then stories with history, next geography, including maps (SBJ: 13–14). Looking back at these early years, Lewis recalls: "I was living almost entirely in my imagination . . . I was training myself to be a novelist." (SBJ: 15. Walter Hooper has edited these childhood stories and published them as *Boxen: The Imaginary World of the Young C. S. Lewis*.)

In many ways, these childhood years were the most idyllic of Lewis's life. Life at home approached the ideal. Albert's successful law practice meant the family was spared financial worry, and later enabled him to send the boys to boarding schools. Indeed, even at Oxford, Jack continued to received regular support from his father. The stability of the family centered around his mother, who had a "talent for happiness" and a cool, logical mind; the perfect counterbalance for the warm, emotional Welsh nature of his father (SBJ: 3). The close bond between Jack and Warren, and the presence of Lizzie Endicott, their nurse who was good to the core, only added to the happiness in the home.

Lewis in School

Of course, Jack and his brother Warnie (Warren) had more to do than just write and draw pictures. Their parents were educated and believed in giving their children the same foundation. Before he reached the age of ten, Jack was already learning Greek and Latin from his mother and other tutors. But when she came down with cancer and soon died in 1908, the first great tragedy came to the little family. Jack believed that God had failed him by not answering his prayers for the recovery of his mother. And his father did not know how to manage his own grief well enough to help his sons through their loss, so a separation developed there as well. It was Jack and Warnie against the world. Finally, the death of his mother left a scar that would take years to heal: the biographers tell us that the grief and fear Jack felt when he saw his mother's corpse led to a fear of emotion itself. Only much later did he realize that the heart was often quicker to grasp meaning than the mind.

Fortunately, these experiences did not prevent Jack's education from going forward, even if the schools his father sent him to were not always the best. In fact, the first boarding school (which Lewis later called "Belsen," the name of a concentration camp) closed soon after the headmaster was certified as insane. Fortunately, Jack, after many pleas to his father, had already been removed from Wynyard and sent to another school. And yet, looking back, he had to admit that he had benefited from kind teachers who had really cared for their students, and from being sent to churches led by pastors who really did believe in the doctrines of the church and preached them openly from the pulpit.

One might conclude from these circumstances that Jack came to hate school even while he was being confirmed in his faith, but that wasn't the case. He did continue to develop intellectually (though school environments were often extremely uncomfortable to him, especially the emphasis upon sports and the way the older students exploited the younger), but the sermons he heard convinced him that he could never measure up to God's standards. So when the matron at Cherbourg, his third school, exposed him to occultism, he willingly abandoned his faith for the freedom of believing in "spirit" with no moral strings attached.

This trend of increasing intellectual development with a corresponding spiritual decay continued under W. T. Kirkpatrick, who had already helped Warren prepare for entrance to the Royal Military Academy at Sandhurst. Jack affectionately called him "the Great Knock" and from him he learned to speak and think carefully, skills that stood him in good stead for the rest of his life. He also adopted his mentor's atheism. (Although to his credit, Kirkpatrick did put on a better suit when he worked in his garden on Sundays!)

Lewis at Oxford

His studies in Kirkpatrick's home (Jack was the only student) included more Greek and Latin, plus French, German, and Italian, not to mention English literature. All this curriculum was meant to prepare him for Oxford, and Kirkpatrick succeeded. Jack was admitted to that prestigious university in 1917 and excelled in the comprehensive examinations that marked the middle (1920) and the end (1922) of his *Literae Humaniores*; a four year degree program in the Greek and Roman classics, philosophy, and ancient history. He then took top honors the very next year in English language and literature, a degree program that usually required two years (Hooper, *C. S. Lewis. A Companion and Guide*: 771).

Lewis doesn't say nearly as much about these studies at Oxford compared to his earlier schools, so his experiences there must have been more positive. But he did recall being so tired that death seemed an attractive option at the time. And his time at Oxford was complicated by the fact that he began his studies there just as World War I got underway. As a citizen of Ireland, he didn't have to enlist, but felt it was his patriotic duty. While waiting for orders, he became friends with his roommate Edward "Paddy" Moore, whose divorced mother Janie and twelve year old sister Maureen lived nearby. Lewis greatly enjoyed their company, and during a visit just before being sent to the front, promised to look after them if anything happened to Paddy.

They were sent to France in 1917, where Paddy was killed in action, after fighting very bravely, being wounded, captured, escaping, and finally shot again, this time fatally. Lewis honored his promise, and Mrs. Moore was in his care for the rest of her life. Jack experienced "trench fever," recovered after three weeks, returned to the front, was hit by shrapnel in four different places (Hooper, *C. S. Lewis*: 11). He was later to recall that while being treated in France, champagne was the only thing he could stomach for a time. But after regaining his health, he found he had lost all taste for it for the rest of his life.

But what could Lewis do with all that education, not to mention a woman in her forties, her daughter, a cook, and a maid? Kirkpatrick had praised Lewis in a letter to his father as one of the most brilliant students he had ever tutored, but also commented that he didn't see many career options for him except in an academic setting. Providentially, Lewis was asked to fill in for one of his tutors who was away for a year, and after that, he was offered a position teaching English in Magdalene College (Hooper, *C. S. Lewis*: 12–13). Lewis realized English suited his temperament better than philosophy, and English language and literature became his academic "home" until his retirement.

A fertile imagination, love of stories, anthropomorphic animals, a mind of unusual capacity – the raw materials were all there. They would be enriched by an education stretching from Lewis's own time to the origin of the English language; and farther back still to ancient Greece and Rome, whose literature is the foundation of western civilization. And his education enabled Lewis to read all these in their original languages. Few students today, even those from wealthy families, are able to enjoy the opportunities that helped shape Lewis. But all these needed a catalyst to bring them together and give them direction. And that catalyst was the Christian faith. But what persuaded Lewis to leave the atheism of his late teens and twenties?

The Path to Faith

Lewis's journey to faith has been thoroughly examined by several biographers (I especially recommend Downing's book *The Most Reluctant Convert*), so a summary here will suffice. Imagine a shopper picking up a new electronic device of some sort, carefully inspecting it to see how it works, its features, etc., and then deciding it's not quite what he needs. This, figuratively speaking, is what Lewis was doing with the philosophies of his time. To his credit, he really wanted to know the meaning of life. He was searching in all the wrong places, but he was searching, and each wrong "article" at least showed him where the answers wouldn't be found.

Romanticism gave way to Kirkpatrick's rationalism for a time, then the lure of the occult tugged at him once more, but the fear of ghosts and who knows what else drove him back in the direction of materialism, where there was nothing supernatural to fear. Meanwhile, MacDonald's *Phantastes* brought to him the "bright shadow" of holiness; "for the first time the song of the sirens sounded like the voice of my mother or my nurse" (SBJ: 179). And Chesterton (*The Everlasting Man*) chimed in with the logic of holiness. His defenses were being broken down and Lewis began to wonder if the defense of his atheism was a lost cause.

As Lewis came to know many of his fellow students and then faculty colleagues at Oxford, some of them became instrumental in his journey to faith. Lewis credited Owen Barfield for exposing his "chronological snobbery," meaning his tendency to accept the latest trends in thought while assuming that what is no longer in vogue must have been discredited (SBJ: 207). Another student, Nevill Coghill, stood out as the most intelligent and well-informed student in a discussion class, and yet was a Christian. Another attack came from a most unexpected direction; the most hard-boiled atheist Lewis ever knew exclaimed during a visit to Lewis's room that the evidence for the historicity of the gospels was very strong. Lewis was shaken ... if *this* person had to own up to the facts (though he never did become a believer), was there something to Christianity after all?

The next step, oddly enough, came on a bus. Lewis felt he was standing before a door, and was free to open it or not. God offered no promises for either choice; he revealed no consequences. Lewis chose to open it. Not long after, in the Trinity Term of 1929, he knelt and admitted that God indeed did exist. Two more years passed before the deist Lewis became the Christian Lewis, and Lewis himself wrote that he was not sure why his belief in Jesus as the Christ came when it did; on a motorcycle ride with Warren to the Whipsnade zoo on September 28, 1931. (How fast was his brother driving?!) The rest is mystery; the biographers can only uncover so much.

The conversion of Lewis was a wonderful event; as is the conversion of anyone to faith in Christ. But did he receive preferential treatment? When he did kneel that night in his rooms at Oxford, he described himself as "the most dejected and reluctant convert in all England ... darting his eyes in every direction for a chance of escape" (SBJ: 228–9). Did

God bring Lewis to himself against his own will? If so, do we really have wills of our own; can we make genuine choices? And why doesn't God give others the same treatment so that they also can find salvation?

Perhaps the answer lies in Lewis's own autobiography. He searched for years to discover the source of joy he had felt since childhood, and he really did want to know the truth about himself and the universe. The search led him through many philosophies, myths, and religions; who would go to so much trouble unless he really wanted the truth? "Seek and you shall find," Jesus promised. Lewis certainly did that, rejecting one way after another, until a gracious God finally responded.

The Christian Lewis

When Lewis became a Christian, the impulse to write remained, though his ambition to be a famous poet faded away. Lewis continued to be a scholar of English language and literature, and wrote several academic works in his chosen subject area. But he wrote far more in service of his faith. The more he wrote, the more he needed to write, for readers all over the English speaking world (and even some who were not native English speakers) came to regard him as their spiritual mentor who could give them advice. Lewis took this responsibility seriously, and responded (sometimes with Warren's help) to everyone who wrote.

As Lewis matured in his faith and as his knowledge of the Scriptures deepened, a great many things about his world troubled him as he looked around at it from a Christian perspective. A chief concern was the assumption in England that Christianity was passé; it had been "tried" and now it was time to move on to something else. But Christianity hadn't been disproved, Lewis discovered; more than any other way it made sense of the world. It certainly had done that for Lewis and he set about explaining and defending the faith in what he surely knew was a losing effort.

Taken together, the correspondence, articles, and books Lewis wrote about Christianity fall (roughly speaking) into three related categories: speaking prophetically to his world, reaching out to non-believers (evangelism), and living the faith while helping others do the same. These categories overlap to some extent, and the contents of any given article or book may fall into more than one category, but these distinctions will prove useful for the discussion of Lewis's theology in the chapters that follow.

Lewis as Prophet

Christianity made sense to Lewis because it explained so much about himself and his world. Lewis studied a wide range of subjects through the lens of his faith: education, space travel, pain, literature, evolution, the priesthood, love, joy, Christmas, family life, courtesy, history, war, sex, animals, music, culture, marriage, and many others. These themes and many more are scattered throughout his books, articles, and letters, especially *The Abolition of Man, The Problem of Pain*, the articles collected in *God in the Dock* and *The World's Last Night and Other Essays*, and "De Descriptione Temporum," his inaugural address at Cambridge University.

In these books and essays the prophetic Lewis speaks to his times. Just as the Old Testament prophets were raised up by God to call their people back to God, so Lewis points out the many idolatries and falsehoods that are infecting the institutions and values of western cultures because the truths of Scripture have been forgotten and replaced by more "modern" ways of thinking. In this role Lewis was doing what believers are called to do: be salt and light to the world.

Lewis as Evangelist

Lewis believed that Christ was the only way to salvation and he used a variety of approaches to convey the message of redemption that have proven effective. In particular he described the power of myth in his own life and explained how he came to regard Christianity as myth that entered into history. It was only natural for him to identify the most important events in the redemption story and use them to construct similar stories. The effectiveness of this subtle approach lies in its appeal to the heart and the imagination, as stories about dying and resurrecting gods in cultures in many times and places have shown. They simply have universal appeal, and in this way Lewis could reach people (as he himself had been prepared) who would draw back from a more direct call to "come forward and be saved."

Till We Have Faces is one example of the story approach, written late in Lewis's life and benefiting from his wife's contributions. Many readers have told me that there were parts they didn't understand when they closed the book. But everyone can feel the pain of the woman telling the story (her name was Orual). The gods gave her a sister (Psyche) she deeply loved, and then cruelly took her away, leaving her with a brutal and coarse father and her own physical ugliness. Lewis knew that people tend to blame God for bringing evil into their lives, or at least allowing it and then not doing anything about it when he could. After all, he is omnipotent or all-powerful – so the theologians tell us – and can do whatever he wishes. But when the readers identify with Orual's plight, Lewis draws them into his net more effectively than by using theological arguments. Orual finally gets her opportunity to present her case to the divine court, and discovers that they have been kind and merciful all along, and that her sister has found complete joy in her new life with them. Lewis both defends God and challenges the readers to examine their own lives. Hence the title; only when a person is willing to show God his true face (self) will God reveal himself in turn. Now that the way is open for honest communication with God, the readers are ready for the salvation message.

Lewis chose more modern types of fiction to prepare others for the gospel message because he knew from his enjoyment of myths just how powerful stories could be. Science fiction was a genre he enjoyed, and since people weren't writing the kind of stories he liked, he and J. R. R. Tolkien, his colleague at Oxford, decided to write some of their own. The plot of *Perelandra*, the second book of the space trilogy (*Out of the Silent Planet* is the first volume; *That Hideous Strength* the third), unfolds on another planet (Venus) and the essential message of the gospel story is imprinted on the imagination of every reader: a sacrifice is made (the hero's name is Ransom) to save a world.

The same can be said of the atoning death of Aslan in *The Lion, the Witch and the Wardrobe*, the first of seven volumes known as *The Chronicles of Narnia. The Chronicles* first appeared in 1950, but their real beginning was much earlier, when Lewis was about sixteen. A picture of a faun (a mythological creature with the body of a goat and head of a man) carrying an umbrella and parcels in a snowy wood "came" to Lewis, and some twenty-four years later, he decided to base a story on that image. Soon, Aslan the lion "came bounding" into the story (Lewis had been dreaming about lions around that time) and he "pulled the whole story together, and soon He pulled the six other Narnian stories in after Him" ("It All Began With A Picture" in OOW: 42). Not only did Lewis use small details from the gospels in *Perelandra* and *The Lion, the Witch and the Wardrobe*, such as the Aramaic words Jesus uttered while on the cross, he even alluded to Old Testament passages that foretell events in the suffering and death of Jesus.

In *Mere Christianity* and in the essays, dialogues, and letters collected by Walter Hooper and published as *God in the Dock*, Lewis replaced the "story" approach with a more direct approach to evangelism based on logic. Lewis got off on the right foot when he decided to "recommend" Christianity to his countrymen. His goal was to bring people to faith in Christ, not get them to join a certain denomination. That approach would have set members of different denominations against each other, while Lewis correctly perceived that the real issue was to persuade people that they needed Christ. After entering the main "hall" of "mere" Christianity, they could enter from there into one of the many Christian "rooms" (churches) that seemed in their opinion to uphold most faithfully what a Christian should believe and how a Christian should live (MC: xi).

Now comes the hard part: what one approach will apply to people of different cultures around the world? Lewis believed there was something humans have in common: a sense of fair play or decent behavior – morality, if you will. And so he began with quarrels; the sort of disputes that result when someone feels wronged and tries to convince the other person of that fact. But the conviction of being wronged, Lewis argues, is possible only if humans have a standard of right and wrong that tells them when they have been treated unjustly. So, Lewis concludes, there must be an external standard of appropriate behavior toward others that everyone accepts. If not, quarrels would not even be possible.

But do people and cultures everywhere agree upon this moral "law?" Certainly, there are individuals who seem to lack a conscience, just as there are people who are color blind. But will we find an entire culture that prizes cowardice over bravery, dishonesty over truthfulness, and selfishness over generosity? Of course not, Lewis argues. Moreover, Lewis adds, even though cultures everywhere agree on the moral law, they often fail to obey that law. Other laws, such as the law of gravity, must be obeyed. But not the law of morality, and that sets it apart.

What significance did Lewis see in this unique law? He believed that it could help decide a question that thinkers have asked since history began. Is the universe simply an accident or the expression of a powerful intelligence? If the latter, then the natural sciences will not discover that power as a fact in the universe any more than the architect of a house could be a wall or floor in that house (MC: 19). But that power could show itself by putting within us an influence that tells us how we ought to behave, and that is exactly what the moral law does.

This law also tells us about its author, and the news may not be to our liking! The law is hard and unyielding, telling us to do the right thing even when acting morally may be painful or dangerous. Moreover, "If God is like the Moral Law, then He is not soft" (MC: 25). If an impersonal mind is behind the law, then we can't expect it to give us any slack. But if God is a personal and a good God, as the law suggests, then he must hate much of what we do, or fail to do. Either way, Lewis concludes, humanity is at odds with the moral law and the source of that law.

When Lewis began his apology for Christianity with the subject of quarrels, he found a way to demonstrate the moral law that everyone could understand. And what sensible person would claim to have always obeyed that law? By inescapable logic, Lewis brought his radio audience to the realization that everyone needs the help that Christianity offers – forgiveness and grace to live a new and better life for those who are willing to confess their failures and accept God's redemption.

Permit me a brief digression. On the way to this conclusion, Lewis introduced another theme that will get major billing in his writings: the awesome holiness of God. I think he did this for two reasons: the Scriptures teach it and Lewis was concerned that many believers had replaced it with a mushy "God is love" theology that makes God so agreeable that sin hardly matters any more. But Lewis isn't having any of this; he knows full well that "our God is a consuming fire" (Heb 12:29).

> God is the only comfort, He is also the supreme terror: the thing we most need and the thing we most want to hide from... - Some people talk as if meeting the gaze of absolute goodness would be fun. They need to think again. They are still only playing with religion. Goodness is either the great safety or the great danger – according to the way you react to it. And we have reacted the wrong way. (MC: 24)

Lewis believed a sense of conviction was just what the doctor ordered for modern England. A few years after these radio addresses he wrote that one of the greatest obstacles to his attempts to promote Christianity was

> the almost total absence from the minds of my audience of any sense of sin... The early Christian preachers could assume in their hearers, whether Jews... or Pagans, a sense of guilt... The ancient man approached God (or even the gods) as the accused man approaches his judge. For the modern man the roles are reversed. He is the judge: God is in the dock... I am very far from believing that I have found the solution of this problem. ("God in the Dock" in GID: 243–4)

There were other obstacles as well. Would logic based upon quarrels reach the atheist, a conviction Lewis knew about firsthand? Perhaps it would convince some, but it didn't convince Lewis. But looking back after his conversion, he came to believe that the quarrel approach did have something to say to the atheist, and might have helped him in his search for God if someone had explained it to him. In brief, Lewis rejected the idea of God because there was so much evil and injustice in the world. It was easier to believe the universe came about by accident. But quarrels reveal the existence of a moral law, and the atheist has no explanation for that. "If the whole universe has no meaning, we should never have found out that it has no meaning: just as, if there were no light in the universe and therefore no creatures with eyes, we should never know it was dark" (MC: 31).

Supposing Lewis was successful in his apologetics – what then? He knew that to point people to Christianity also meant sending them to the Bible for spiritual nourishment, and once there, the new believer would soon read about miraculous events. Nor is there any way out of the problem, for the resurrection of Jesus is at the heart of the Christian faith. The problem then is to defend miracles to people who live in a very scientific age and expect to find rational explanations for every event.

When Lewis wrote about the Moral Law that cultures everywhere recognize, he contrasted the Moral Law which can be (and often is!) disobeyed with the "laws of nature," such as gravity, which we are not free to ignore. Since the natural world is governed by these laws, and since these laws cannot be broken, should we reject the Biblical accounts of miracles that seem to break nature's laws?

Lewis seems to work against himself by granting the point; laws are "necessary truths" and no miracle can break them. But Lewis finds the laws of nature do not *cause* events to happen and never have. Rather, "they state the pattern to which every event – if only it can be induced to happen – must conform" (M: 60). If someone drops an object, the law of gravity determines what will happen. But the object must first be dropped; only then does the law of gravity operate. In the same way, Lewis observes, if God decides to create a miraculous spermatozoon in the body of a virgin, the laws of nature "at once take it over" and nine months later, a child is born (M: 60–1). By definition, then, a miracle is an event which is caused by God, and the results follow natural laws.

Lewis as Believer and Mentor

First, Lewis wanted to understand Christianity. His conversion didn't answer all his questions, but it opened the door to the Scriptures and two thousand years of church history, and Lewis spent the rest of his life reflecting upon what the Scriptures revealed and how the great Christian minds before him had understood them. In my professional opinion, his personal studies, judging by what he wrote, reveal him to be a very accomplished amateur theologian. And his theology led to practics. Once, when Lewis was having lunch with Owen Barfield and a pupil, he referred to philosophy as a "subject." "It wasn't a subject to Plato," responded Barfield, "it was a way" (SBJ: 225). Lewis took that remark to heart, and a good deal of his writing is concerned with how he tried to live what he believed and how he encouraged and guided others to do the same.

The Four Loves is a good example of Christian instruction. Here Lewis shows how affection, friendship, and erotic love each need God's agape love (*charity* in the King James translation) to support them so they can contribute to our lives as God intended. In *Letters to Malcomb: Chiefly on Prayer* Lewis offers advice to new believers, including examples from his own prayer life. Even more advice (and warnings) comes through the imaginary correspondence of *The Screwtape Letters*. *Reflections on the Psalms* offers both practical advice on Christianity as a way and thoughtful analysis of the meaning of selected psalms. Finally, Lewis reflected on the Biblical implications of Christ descending into Hades in *The Great Divorce*. The implications of his views of Purgatory will be explored in chapter six.

Lewis the prophet, Lewis the evangelist, Lewis the spiritual mentor to others...join me now for a closer look into these three perspectives of the theology of this amazing person. First, we'll survey the history of the West to discover how our own times compare with the ages that are past. Next, we'll learn why the redemptive work of Christ is the key to understanding Lewis's imaginative works. And finally, join me for a journey on a bus ride to the spirit world with our mentor, and his mentor and tour guide, that will give us a glimpse of spiritual perfection as Lewis portrayed it.

Chapter 2

Lewis Looks at His World

"Eustace had turned into a dragon while he slept."
Illustration © 2007 by Deborah Wilson Camp

Poor Eustace! "He thought for a second that yet another dragon was staring up at him out of the pool. But in an instant he realized the truth. That dragon face in the pool was his own reflection. There was no doubt of it. It moved as he moved: it opened and shut its mouth as he opened and shut his.

He had turned into a dragon while he was asleep. Sleeping on a dragon's hoard with greedy, dragonish thoughts in his heart, he had become a dragon himself."

(VDT: 74–5)

How did Eustace come to be in such a state? Lewis thinks it was the way he was raised; by very modern parents whom Eustace called by their first names. He liked animals, especially beetles that were dead and pinned on cards, and he liked books of information with pictures of grain elevators. And the one lovely picture in the whole house was kept out of sight a in back room! In brief, there was very little fun, or pleasure, or beauty in that house. So it's not surprising that Lucy and Edmund were not looking forward to staying with Eustace, whose parents were their uncle and aunt; nor is it surprising at all that when Eustace found himself in Narnia with Lucy and Edmund that he proved to be very poor company indeed.

Now the reason Lewis described the upbringing of poor Eustace as he did was because he felt a person's education was very important. Modern schools and modern parents and modern textbooks were a concern to Lewis because all too often, the children who were exposed to them resembled Eustace in many ways. When Lewis came across a high school textbook of English literature, the philosophy of the use of language he found therein confirmed his misgivings and concerned him so much he responded with *The Abolition of Man*.

Aesthetics and Morality in the "Green Book"

Lewis never gave the names of the authors or the title of the high school textbook that concerned him; he simply referred to it as the "Green Book." It was *The Control of Language: A Critical Approach to Reading and Writing*, by Alex King and Martin Ketley, published in 1939. Lewis takes up where the authors of the "Green Book" are discussing the famous English poet Samuel Taylor Coleridge (1772–1834), who overheard two tourists looking at a waterfall. One tourist said it was pretty, and the other sublime. Coleridge silently rejected the first opinion and agreed with the second. But the authors of the textbook wrote that when the person said the waterfall was sublime, he was not really making a remark about the waterfall but about *his own feelings*. And the authors added: "This confusion is continually present in language as we use it. We appear to be saying something very important about something: and actually we are only saying something about our own feelings" (AOM: 14).

At first glance, this all seems innocent enough and many readers would pass on without really noticing. In fact, that is a big part of the problem; few students in their teens would even realize that objective values were being reclassified as subjective feelings. But Lewis grasped what the authors were really saying and he realized how serious the implications were. Values, the authors claimed, are nothing more than subjective expressions of personal feelings. This can lead to deconstructionism – what the original author intended to say is lost, since all language is arbitrary and since the reader will impose his or her own perspective upon the text. Carried to the extreme, the meaning of the reader is more important than the meaning of the author.

Lewis emphatically rejected this line of thinking. Beyond what an author intended to say, there are objective values, language can be used to express them, and people need to be trained to recognize those values. "Until quite modern times all teachers and even all men believed the universe to be such that certain emotional reactions on our part could be either congruous or incongruous to it – believed, in fact, that objects did not merely receive, but could *merit*, our approval or disapproval, our reverence, or our contempt" (AOM: 25).

In other words, Lewis is saying, the man who called the waterfall sublime was not trying to describe his emotions and nothing more; he was claiming that what he was admiring merited those emotions. But such feelings are not merely instinctive. It is dangerous to assume that people will on their own recognize beautiful art or good literature. The explorers who first came upon the Grand Canyon viewed it not as a spectacle of beauty and grandeur, but as nothing more than an obstacle to their progress. If schools do not include aesthetics in their curriculum, the arts will suffer and students will be impoverished. If pupils are taught that their feelings and viewpoints are what matter, they will be cut off from the great minds of the past.

But there is much more at stake here than the capacity to recognize good literature, music, or art. Lewis maintains that training in aesthetics lays the groundwork for moral formation. He quotes Traherne: "Can you be righteous unless you be just in rendering to things their due esteem?" (Thomas Traherne, English mystical prose writer, poet, and divine [1637–74], from *Centuries of Meditations*, 1. 12: 26). Lewis also agrees with Aristotle, who held that the aim of education is to make the pupil like and dislike what he ought (*Nicomachean Ethics* 1104 B; AOM: 26).

Lewis explains that in all ancient civilizations and up to the present (in most countries) there has always been agreement on the *doctrine of objective value*: the belief that in response to what the universe is, and what humans are, there are attitudes that are really true, and attitudes that are wrong or false. This means that reactions to beauty (or its lack), that is, emotions or sentiments about what we see or hear, can be *reasonable*. They correspond to an *external reality*, and so an appropriate emotion reveals something about that external object. But the textbook that Lewis objected to so strenuously taught that an emotion was only an emotional expression, not in agreement or disagreement with Reason. In the system of objective value, a person may err in not giving something its due esteem, or in giving esteem to something or someone who does not deserve it. But if emotions do not reflect external reality, they can't even rise "to the dignity of error!" (AOM: 30).

Lewis explains this modern view of feelings, known as subjectivism, in more detail in his essay "The Poison of Subjectivism." Value judgments, it turns out, are not judgments at all, according to subjectivism. "They are sentiments, or complexes, or attitudes, produced in a community by the pressure of its environment and its traditions, and differing from one community to another. To say that a thing is good is merely to express our feeling about it; and our feeling about it is the feeling we have been socially conditioned to have" (in CR: 73).

This view of reality strikes at the core of a person. The intellect or spirit of a man must be joined to the animal body by the "chest" – his heart or emotions. Only then is he fully human. But when the heart is unable to connect to the objective truth outside of him, which is the source of all value judgments (Lewis refers to it as the Tao), the result is "men without chests;" people who lack the capacity for moral development. Eustace is a perfect example; he is a "boy without a chest" and must "undergo a kind of death" to be reborn into humanity (Jacobs, *The Narnian*: 209).

Lewis published *The Abolition of Man* in 1947, and gave his inaugural Cambridge address in 1954. A few years later, confirmation for his views came from across the English Channel in 1968. Francis Schaeffer, founder of the L'Abri Fellowship in Switzerland, was also concerned about the direction of change in western culture. For him, the divide began in Germany, around 1890, and spread from there through Europe, then England, and finally the United States (*The God Who is There*: 14–16).

Until that time, as Lewis also recognized, people always believed there were absolutes in knowledge and morality. Philosophers reasoned by cause and effect until Hegel, who proposed a different path: thesis, antithesis, and finally synthesis. Then came Kierkegaard, who believed human reason could not reach a synthesis; a leap of faith was required. Before long, art became random, as Van Gogh, Gauguin, and Cezanne expressed the outlook of philosophy that all is chance; there is no ultimate meaning in life. Music followed next, beginning with Debussy and ultimately descending to musique concrete, notes distorted by a machine; and the random sounds of John Cage. And so on through drama, literature, and finally into theology.

Two different approaches from two different thinkers, but they lead to the same conclusion: there has been a change in the way we come to truth, think about truth, and attain truth, or fail to do so. And that change has now permeated all of western thought and life, and left a legacy of despair. The universe is silent, God is dead, or at least silent, and the only "authentic" life for a person is to act in whatever way seems right.

Aesthetics and Morality in That Hideous Strength

Here is a brief summary of *That Hideous Strength*. In the third volume of the science fiction trilogy, Mark and Jane Studdock, a young, modern couple, find themselves caught up in a sinister plot to overthrow England. The National Institute for Coordin-ated Experiments (NICE), under the leadership of Frost and Wither, and guided by fallen angels, is manipulating public opinion by the press, seizing control of local governments, and planning to dominate the entire world. NICE is even attempting to conquer death itself by scientific means. So far, their research appears to be successful in keeping alive a head detached from its body; the first step in becoming free from the body and eventually removing all organic life from the earth. Eventually, Mark is chosen to be the next head, but first he must be conditioned to follow orders without thinking . . .

To achieve this conditioning, the leaders of NICE bring Mark to the Objective Room. In this context Lewis again stresses the connection between aesthetics and morality. The proportions of the room were all wrong. The arched door was off center. There are many paintings in the room, including several with scriptural subjects. But all of them seem warped in one way or another. Here is a woman with hair inside her mouth, there a depiction of the Last Supper with bugs crawling around. A stranger is standing between a painting of Christ and Lazarus. A giant mantis is playing a fiddle while being eaten by another mantis. There are the spots on the ceiling and the table that don't seem to form a pattern – or do they? Mark feels most uncomfortable when asked to climb up a ladder, touch one of the spots on the ceiling, climb back down, and then repeat the process again and again.

Day after day Mark is brought to this room until he begins to understand the point of it all. By "objectivity" NICE meant the state where "all specifically human reactions were killed in a man" (THS: 299). But Mark began to react to the room in a way NICE didn't anticipate.

As the desert first teaches men to love water, or as absence first reveals affection, there rose up against this background of the sour and the crooked some kind of vision of the sweet and the straight. Something else – something he vaguely called the "Normal" – apparently existed.... He was not thinking in moral terms at all; or else (what is much the same thing) he was having his first deeply moral experience. (THS: 299)

A few days later, things come to a climax. When Mark enters the Objective Room he sees that the table has been moved back to the wall and in its place is a wooden cross on the floor, almost life size. Frost commands him to insult the cross and to step on (Lewis uses the word "trample") the face of the figure on the cross. But Mark began to shrink back... even though he had never believed in Christianity, if it was mere superstition, why did they want him to step on the cross? He thought about Jesus, who died complaining that he had been forsaken. But was that a reason to reject him? "Supposing the Straight was utterly powerless, always and everywhere certain to be mocked, tortured, and finally killed by the Crooked, what then? Why not go down with the ship?" (THS: 337).

Mark had long ago realized that he was not going to leave NICE alive; no one ever did. He was trapped. But with the introduction of the cross, the situation became more complicated than just the normal and the crooked, and the stakes were higher than his own life. "If I take a step in any direction," he thought, "I may step over a precipice" (THS: 335). Frost continues to urge him to obey, but Mark refuses. In two wonderful double entendres, he replies: "It's all *bloody* nonsense, and *I'm damned* if I do any such thing" (THS: 337).

Yes, he certainly would be... Mark was to *trample* upon the figure on the cross; Lewis's way of recalling Heb 10:29, which warns against "trampling underfoot the Son of God, and regarding as unclean the blood of the covenant." If someone can be conditioned to accept perversion in the arts, what is warped, base, and twisted at last ceases to provoke any reaction at all. Soon, moral perversion will also be acceptable, and ultimately the destiny of the soul is at stake.

Aesthetics and God in Reflections on the Psalms

As a new believer, Lewis regularly turned to the Scriptures after his return to Christianity and soon got the impression from the Psalms that God was an insecure egotist, constantly telling us to praise him. What he most wanted was to be told that he was good and great. Lewis solved this problem when he realized that many objects in nature, literature, and art deserve, or merit (demand?), our admiration. Others most definitely do not. The goodness and quality we admire in art and literature have their source in God himself. "He is that Object to admire which (or, if you like, to appreciate which) is simply to be awake, to have entered the real world; not to appreciate which is to have lost the greatest experience, and in the end to have lost all" (ROP: 92).

Lewis is making the point that as fallen creatures, people need the "training" provided in the Psalms. They reveal the character of God and the appropriate response to that character, just as a good education trains young people in the proper response to the arts. Even in mathematics and the empirical sciences, beauty and truth, beauty and solutions also go hand in hand, reflecting the beauty and wisdom of the Designer expressed in the design of the universe.

To go in the other direction, to buy into the perspective of the Green Book, is to remove objective value from the universe, and substitute our own emotional impulses. Nature herself will become "mere Nature"; no longer a portrayer of objective truth or "facthood," but simply an instrument for some people to use to control others. Finally, even human nature itself will fall victim to "mere nature," for the more nature is defeated, the more strength it gains (Foster, "An Estimation of an Admonition:" 420–1).

Should Lewis have been so concerned about a textbook? One high school textbook by itself is not that far-reaching in its influence, but on the other hand, its significance lies in the fact that the authors were reflecting a very popular viewpoint of their times. Lewis himself was surrounded by subjectivists when he began teaching at Cambridge University in 1954. Professors such as F. R. Leavis rejected the objective standards that Lewis believed cultures everywhere recognized, and so Lewis found himself once again battling for the values that could prepare a person for Christianity, just as he had fought so long for Christianity itself (Hooper, *C. S. Lewis*: 73–4).

Lewis at Cambridge

When Lewis did come to Cambridge to occupy the chair of English that had been established for him, his inaugural address revealed the scope of his concern about the recent changes in the way we perceive or fail to perceive the truth. To highlight the significance of these changes, Lewis hit upon a brilliant approach; one that few others would be qualified to manage. He looked at the entire sweep of western civilization and then identified several periods of changes so major that historians use them today to distinguish between ages. In this way he could compare the most recent period of major changes, the changes that concerned him, and show how they were different, and potentially more far-reaching in their influence, than any previous time of change.

The first significant historical division he described marked the transition from Antiquity to the Dark Ages: the fall of the Roman Empire, the barbarian invasions, and the christening of Europe (SLE: 4). These were huge changes indeed, and mostly in terms of losses. Yet the survival of Latin enabled the disciplines of law and rhetoric to survive and even prosper during the Dark Ages. The codex replaced the scroll (*volumen*), making possible more precise scholarship, and the invention of the stirrup contributed much to the "art of war" (SLE: 6).

The next major shift saw the Dark Ages giving way to the Middle Ages around the twelfth century. Things begin to improve: there were new architectural solutions such as the flying buttress, the recovery of the text of Aristotle from the Arabs, which greatly influenced the *Summa Theologica* of Thomas Aquinas, and new forms of poetry (rhymed and syllabic verse). And yet Lewis finds greater change elsewhere.

Next, Lewis considered the dawning of the sciences in the seventeenth century. Copernicus finally convinced most people that the earth was not at the center of the solar system, a giant step forward in astronomy. Larger and better lenses also benefited astronomy, and the Royal Society was founded in England. Now science had become a genie that could never be put back into her bottle (my metaphor, not Lewis's), but the by-products that would transform the West were still to come (SLE: 6–7).

But after giving all of these "divides" their due, Lewis concludes that none of them can compare with the radical changes of the last two centuries, changes that were still continuing in his lifetime and were even accelerating. In politics, *rulers* are being replaced by *leaders*. Where citizens once hoped for justice and incorruption, now leaders are chosen on the basis of charisma, excitement, and "soundbites." In the arts, modern poetry (sometimes incomprehensible even to other poets), music, abstract painting, etc. are unlike anything before. In religion, Christianity is on the way out. Of course, there are still many Christians around. "But the presumption has changed." Religious beliefs and practices are now the exception rather than the norm (SLE: 9).

Finally, Lewis plays his "trump card:" machines. So far-reaching are the effects of machines that for the first time in the history of the world our place in nature has been changed. Passing over the enormous economic and social consequences, Lewis turns to the way machines (perhaps *technology* would be the word we would use today) have influenced the way we think. We now want and shop for the "latest," what is "new and improved." Machines are continually improved (hence lending indirect support to the theory of evolution) and so we have become *consumers*. Getting new and better appliances is the idea, not preserving what we have.

The Post-Christian West

Lewis was careful not to offend his scholarly audience at Cambridge, but as a Christian apologist he didn't just note these changes, he was disturbed by them. The faith he felt called to defend was on its way out. And not just his faith; his "Old Western" culture was on its way out as well. And because he felt more at home on the far side of the "Great Divide," he asked his Cambridge listeners to view him as a specimen. From his perspective, the modern world was increasingly a foreign place, cut off from its roots, and so his convictions had historical value. There is a real poignancy in the words of a man who knew he was nearly obsolete: "Use your specimens while you can. There are not going to be many more dinosaurs" (SLE: 14).

Was the post-Christian West returning to paganism? Not at all, Lewis stated, correcting those who were describing the West in those terms. "A post-Christian man is not a Pagan; you might as well think that a married woman recovers her virginity by divorce" (SLE: 10). When Christianity is abandoned, paganism is also ruled out.

> But roughly speaking we may say that whereas all history was
> for our ancestors divided into two periods, the pre-Christian
> and the Christian ... for us it falls into three – the pre-Christian,
> the Christian and ... the post-Christian. This surely must make
> a momentous difference ... Christians and Pagans had much
> more in common with each other than either has with a post-
> Christian. The gap between those who worship different gods is
> not so wide as that between those who worship and those who
> do not. (SLE: 5)

Lewis didn't want to return to paganism, but at least the
pagans accepted the supernatural and worshipped their gods.
Moreover, the pagan myths that underlie western civilization,
Lewis believed, prepared those cultures for Christianity, when
myth became history. In *The Pilgrim's Regress*, Lewis's first book
as a believer, the allegorical figure History explains to pilgrim
John the value of the mythology of ancient cultures such as
Greece and Rome. "No one is born able to read: so that the
starting point for all of us must be a picture and not the Rules.
And there are more than you suppose who are illiterate all their
lives, or who, at the best, never learn to read well" (PR: 152).

By "Rules" Lewis meant moral codes such as the Torah,
while the pictures were the mythological stories God gave to
the pagans to awaken their desire for him. "He sent the
human race what I call good dreams: I mean those queer
stories scattered all through the heathen religions about a
god who dies and comes to life again and, by his death, has
somehow given new life to men" (MC: 39). When John finally
took the plunge into faith, doubts about the supernatural
assailed him. Then he heard a voice (the voice of God) telling
him:

> Child, if you will, it *is* mythology. It is but truth, not fact: an
> image, not the very real. But then it is My mythology. The
> words of Wisdom are also myth and metaphor: but since they

do not know themselves for what they are, in them the hidden myth is master, where it should be servant: and it is but of man's inventing. But this is My inventing, this is the veil under which I have chosen to appear even from the first until now. For this end I made your senses and for this end your imagination, that you might see My face and live. (TPR: 171)

Yes, the pagans worshipped many idols and strange gods. But they worshipped. Yes, the pagans fell into many kinds of perversions of thought and deed. But they believed in gods, they thanked them for their crops, and sought their guidance and protection. And when Christianity came, Lewis reminds us, the stories they received from God were a good preparation for another story telling how God became flesh, died for humanity, and rose again.

When He created the vegetable world He knew already what dreams the annual death and resurrection of the corn would cause to stir in pious Pagan minds, He knew already that He himself must so die and live again and in what sense, including and far transcending the old religion of the Corn King. ("Miracles" in GID: 37)

But today, in this time of unprecedented change, the old stories have been swept away and replaced by the explanations which science and technology provide. No longer do modern westerners realize that the miracles Christ performed show locally what God does universally every year.

God creates the vine and teaches it to draw up water by its roots, and with the aid of the sun, to turn that water into a juice which will ferment and take on certain qualities. Thus, every year, from Noah's time till ours, God turns water into wine. That, men fail to see . . . they attribute real and ultimate causality to the chemical and other material phenomena which are all that our senses can discover in it. But when Christ at Cana makes water into wine, the mask is off. The miracle has only half its effect if it only convinces us that Christ is God: it will have its full effect if whenever we see a vineyard or drink a glass of wine we remember that here works He who sat at the wedding party at Cana. ("Miracles" in GID: 29)

Yes, "that, men fail to see." It's "Mother Nature" now; things "just happen that way;" the "laws of nature" are working, not divine beings. In tracing these changes in the West, Lewis arrived at the reasons he lived in a post-Christian England. Of course, he knew full well that there were (and are) many believers in his own time. But the key for him was that leaders now increasingly turn to scientists for the answers to social problems, not to the priests. Any ruler, and those they ruled, and not just rulers in the West, in the millennia before the "Great Divide," and many even today, would wonder at the sanity of any culture that depended upon human intelligence to ensure its survival. "Do you not fear the wrath of the gods?" they would ask. "Do you not desire their protection and guidance?" From ancient Sumer, the beginning of civilization, to the day before yesterday, the separation of church and state was unthinkable. But now, as Lewis has observed, "the presumption has changed."

The Christian Viewpoint

In his other writings, Lewis was not so reluctant to express his opinions as he was at Cambridge. As we've seen, modern art, music, and literature are becoming more and more the expression of the artist's feelings or moods. But when Lewis searches the Scriptures, he finds that God's goal for humanity is to help us become more like Christ. We are to imitate him, reflect him, until he is formed in us. Even Christ himself claimed that he did only what he saw the Father doing (John 5:19). Lewis then applied this principle of imitation to literature, and I might add, the same would be true of art and music.

> The basis of all critical theory [is] the maxim that an author should never conceive himself as bringing into existence beauty or wisdom which did not exist before, but simply and solely as trying to embody in terms of his own art some reflection of eternal Beauty and Wisdom. Our criticism . . . would have affinities with the primitive or Homeric theory in which the poet is the mere pensioner of the Muse . . . above all it would be opposed to the idea that literature is self-expression. ("Christianity and Literature" in CR: 7)
>
> For the Christian, then, his own temperament and experiences are not important in themselves, while the unbeliever may focus on them simply because they are his. What matters to the believer is what comes through him from a higher source. Not "is it mine?," but "is it good?" ("Christianity and Literature" in CR: 9)

Collectively, the artistic expressions of any group of people who share a common language and homeland help form the culture of those people. On this "higher" level, Lewis remains consistent to his Christian principles. Culture is not, in itself, held up as something important in the Scriptures. It must, just as individual expressions of art and literature, be subordinated to God, in whom all values reside ("Christianity and Culture" in CR: 26).

The implications of Lewis's review at Cambridge of western history are twofold: a breakdown in structure in the arts and literature, resulting in the loss of ancient and medieval learning, and the systematic exclusion of Christianity from national life. Leaders now turn to scientists instead of priests for the solutions to life's problems. But what is causing these momentous changes? Lewis believed that God reaches out to humanity through myth, but his view of history also reflected the Biblical perspective that fallen angels have a part to play. Lewis speaks to the influence of angels upon human history in *That Hideous Strength*, where under the guise of fiction he could safely reveal his inner convictions.

The Hidden Influence

I noted above that NICE was under the guidance of fallen angels, which Frost and Wither called "macrobes." The word "macrobe" does double service; Lewis avoids turning off the reader who doesn't want Scripture to intrude into science fiction, and he also gives the impression that NICE views them simply as larger microbes rather than spirit beings. Lewis uses MacPhee, one of Ransom's household in *That Hideous Strength* (a logical skeptic probably modeled after Lewis's admired atheist teacher, Kirkpatrick), to give us a different perspective. He describes angels to Jane as "eldils" (the "positive" word for angels in the trilogy) which live in space, can alight on a planet like a bird on a branch, don't breathe or reproduce, and some are "more or less permanently attached to particular planets" (THS: 191). And, of course, some of them associated with our planet are definitely not friendly.

Lewis is faithfully reflecting his faith; the Bible reveals all this and much more about angels. Lewis follows Scripture in depicting Satan as the chief angel over the earth who can offer Jesus all the kingdoms of the world, and then extends the same idea to Venus and Mars, the other planets Ransom visits. These angels, and their planets, are unfallen, and so naturally the plot revolves around the efforts of earth's fallen angels to extend their contagion to the other planets. In *Perelandra*, the second volume of the trilogy, Lewis visited the Garden of Eden, as it were, by depicting the temptation of the Eve of

Venus. Now, back on earth, Lewis uses *That Hideous Strength* to suggest how he imagines the predictions of Scripture might play out as evil makes its final attempt to rule the earth. First Genesis, now Revelation.

Mark, Jane's husband, has been drawn into NICE and the day comes when the leaders take him (to a point) into their confidence. At that very time, in the basement of the head-quarters, a head which has been removed from its body is being kept alive (so they believe) through technology. And through that head's mouth they receive orders from fallen angels. Lewis uses this devil-led organization to reveal some very interesting views which I believe were his own. In ancient times, the leaders of NICE observe, contact with angels was only occasional and hindered by superstitions. Nor had man advanced to the point that angels found us of much interest.

> But though there has been little intercourse, there has been profound influence. Their effect on human history has been far greater than that of the microbes, though, of course, equally unrecognized. In the light of what we now know, *all history will have to be rewritten*. The real causes of all the principal events are quite unknown to historians; that, indeed, is why history has not yet succeeded in becoming a science. (THS: 257; my emphasis)

Is this remarkable view of history Biblical? Lewis does have a Scriptural leg to stand on: when Daniel read the book of Jeremiah and realized that the time of Babylonian exile (70 years) was nearly over, he began praying for God to bring Jeremiah's prophecy to pass. Three weeks later, the archangel Gabriel appeared, and explained the delay by saying he was opposed by the "prince of Persia." Finally, the archangel Michael came to help and Gabriel was able to carry out his mission. As he left Daniel, Gabriel informed him that he was returning to the struggle, and that next the prince of Greece would come. It's only a brief glimpse behind the curtain, so to speak, but the inference is that beneath Satan, the angelic ruler of this world, there are subordinate angels over nations; some fallen, and some not, since Michael is identified as the archangel over Israel (Dan 10:10–21; 12:1).

Since *That Hideous Strength* is Lewis's view of how Biblical prophecy may be realized in the last days, the goals of NICE for the earth arise from a combination of subjectivism, modern science, and the influence of devils. In other words, Lewis was open to the possibility that these factors which he found so alarming might well usher in the end times. First, NICE planned to do away with most humans, since they can be educated only with respect to gaining knowledge. The few who remain will be useful to the macrobes when they have been conditioned to believe that emotions are simply chemical reactions that have no relation to facts (THS: 259). The separation of our emotions from objective reality is precisely what Lewis objected to in *The Abolition of Man*; carried to its extreme, humans will become conditioned to obey the macrobes (fallen angels) without question. "We were only following orders" was the typical plea at the Nuremburg trials. This conditioning almost worked on Mark in the Objective Room, but fortunately, he was able to find the courage to take the side of the good and the straight.

Given his theology-averse readers, Lewis doesn't use words like angels; much less does he directly quote Scripture in the science fiction trilogy. But the attempt of NICE to take over the world and "manage" humanity could be seen as Lewis's version of the end times as described in the book of Revelation. The antichrist and the false prophet of Revelation chapter 13 gain control over humanity for a brief time (and martyr many believers) and they are able to produce miracles because Satan has given them his authority. Satan has found someone who will accept his offer of all the kingdoms of the world; the very same enticement which Jesus refused when Satan came to him in the desert.

One Satanic accomplishment at that time will be, John predicts in the book of Revelation, a mysterious image of the beast (antichrist) who had a mortal wound and yet recovered. The false prophet gives orders for its construction and then somehow gives it breath that enables it to speak (Rev 13:13–15). Lewis expected Satan to deceive humans by using the technology that they rely on. The head detached from its body (Revelation's image of the antichrist) down in the basement of NICE is to all appearances kept alive by technology, but really is able to speak by the agency of the macrobes. Filostrato, the technician who believed his scientific expertise kept the head alive, discovered this when the head spoke even though his equipment was turned off (THS: 354).

Putting it all together, those at NICE represent the "materialistic magician" Lewis described in *The Screwtape Letters*; people who are open to impersonal forces, but reject the idea of spirit beings. By taking technology to its limits, denying the existence of the soul, and rejecting any possibility of the emotions or heart of a person responding to objective truth, such people become the perfect tools of fallen angels who use them to frustrate the purposes of God on earth.

Lewis and Science

Lewis did not view science and the technology it produces as demonic. But his Biblical perspective warned him that in its fallen state, humanity was intelligent enough to know that life ends in death, but not strong enough to endure that knowledge. Not only that, fallen angels are also at work behind the scenes. Yes, Lewis really believed that, and to fully appreciate his world view, both factors must be taken into account. They explain man's inhumanity to man, and our fear of death.

With science as a tool in our hands, Lewis knew it would be used according to who was guiding those hands. He was fascinated by space and even had a telescope at his home, but he adamantly opposed the colonization of other planets, even if the earth does run out of resources. History has already shown many times how we will treat lesser-developed cultures when we want their land. So when Lewis depicted the first encounter between humans and beings on another planet, he made colonization one of the key themes of *Out of the Silent Planet* (OSP).

Here is a brief summary of *Out of the Silent Planet*. The first volume of the science fiction trilogy begins with Elwin Ransom, an Oxford professor of philology, on a walking tour. He meets a woman concerned that her retarded son Harry hasn't returned home, and promises he'll look for him. Soon he comes to a home where he hears a noisy argument, and pushes his way through the hedge to intervene. There he meets Weston, a physicist who has invented a propulsion system for a spacecraft, and Devine, a former classmate. They are trying to persuade Harry by means of alcohol to enter the spaceship for a return voyage to Mars. When they find out that Ransom is unmarried and won't be missed, they abduct him instead.

On Mars, Ransom manages to escape and meets three different intelligent species, all friendly. He learns the language of the planet, and eventually is summoned to meet Oyarsa, the unfallen angel who oversees the planet, just as Satan has charge of this planet. Lewis calls the spirit beings of the planet "eldils;" they correspond to "regular" angels, while Oyarsa would be an angel of higher order. Ransom learns that Mars was attacked some time ago by Satan, but Oyarsa repelled him and confined him to earth. But the planet was damaged in the attack, and its lifespan is nearing its end. Oyarsa sends the three back to earth and alters the ship so that it blows up shortly after landing. Ransom barely escapes in time.

As the plot unfolds, all three earthlings, even Ransom, a nominal Christian modeled after Lewis himself, display the fear that characterizes our planet, in Lewis's view. Devine is after the gold on Mars, but fears the strange looking inhabitants of Mars, as does Ransom. Weston (his name suggests "western") fears the death of his species. He knows the resources of earth will someday be exhausted and mankind will need to reach other planets if the race is to survive. Everyone also fears Oyarsa; in fact, Devine and Weston come all the way back to earth after Oyarsa summons them during their first trip. They intend to get Harry for the sacrifice they suppose Oyarsa wants, and Ransom's interference with their plans cause them to take him instead.

Weston's fear of death makes him quite willing to liquidate inferior species, and he defines "inferior" as any culture less technologically advanced than those of earth. Through Devine's quest for gold and Weston's search for the fountain of youth, figuratively speaking, Lewis neatly sums up the motivations behind the colonization on earth of undeveloped countries by western countries over the past several centuries.

When Ransom learns more about Mars, his fear begins to subside, and he finds that the natives do indeed have the capacity for technology. Since the planet is unfallen, they freely share resources with each other and prefer a simple life in harmony with nature. Big cities, roads, automobiles, etc. are simply unnecessary. And since they do not fear death as on earth, they do not use medical science to prolong life, nor technology to reach other planets before their own planet dies.

Oyarsa finally has his audience with the space travelers. Ransom translates for Weston, who informs the angel "your tribal life with its stone-age weapons... and elementary social structure has nothing to compare with our civilization . . . Our right to supersede you is the right of the higher over the lower" (OSP: 135). Weston believes this "right" is based on survival of the species; life must continue. "Life is greater than any system of morality; her claims are absolute. It is not by tribal taboos and copy-book maxims that she has pursued her relentless march from the amoeba to man and from man to civilization" (OSP: 136).

After further questioning of Weston, with Ransom translating and interpreting, Oyarsa is able to grasp Weston's viewpoints. Through him, Lewis passes judgment on those in our world who believe humanity must survive at any cost.

> I see now how the lord of the silent world (meaning Satan) has bent you. There are laws that all *hnau* (Lewis's word for all species with souls) know, of pity and straight dealing and shame and the like, and one of these is the love of kindred. He has taught you to break all of them except this one, which is not one of the greatest laws; this one he has bent till it becomes folly and has set it up, thus bent, to be a little, blind Oyarsa in your brain. (OSP: 138)

Lewis next exposes the illogic of Weston's loyalty to humanity. Oyarsa points out that he has come to a planet near the end of its lifespan. Yes, Weston says, but he reminds Oyarsa that his efforts are only the first attempt to travel in space. We will go to other planets, he promises. Those will also die, says Oyarsa. Eventually all worlds will die, what then? Weston has no answer. Oyarsa then asks a very interesting question: haven't you wondered why we, on a dying planet, haven't come to conquer your planet? Weston laughs, and, with typical western mindset, tells Oyarsa the beings on his planet don't have the necessary technology to reach other planets. Yes we do, Oyarsa responds; but we are remaining here because we are not afraid of death.

This is too much for Weston. Reaching his breaking point, he shouts at Oyarsa in his pidgin English: "Trash! Defeatist trash! You say your Maledil (God) let all go dead. Other one, Bent One (Satan), he fight, jump, live – not all talkee-talkee. Me no care Maledil. Like Bent One better: me on his side" (OSP: 140).

Now we can tie it all together. The world Lewis saw through Biblical lenses was a complex record of human events made even more complicated by both good and bad influences from the spirit world. Anyone who embraced Christianity as Lewis had would soon discover that he had stepped into a battlefield with human souls at stake, including his own. On the positive side, Lewis also believed that the Bible told how the struggle would play out. Satan will make a final attempt at world domination at the end of the age, but the return of Christ will spell the end of the antichrist and usher in God's kingdom.

When that end would come no one knows, but the significance of Lewis's Cambridge address is that at the peak of his career, he could look over the sweep of western history, and when he did so, he found that he was living in a time of unprecedented change. What perturbed him in the Green Book was happening on a huge scale. And it was part of a plan. Fallen spirits led by Satan, the Oyarsa of this planet, have been and still are working behind the scenes to influence the course of history. The erosion of standards in the arts and literature was being followed by the same decline in morality. Christianity itself was becoming a thing of the past in official circles. He chronicled the development of this erosion in "De Descriptione Temporum," he warned against it in *The Abolition of Man*, and traced its origin to fallen humanity under Satanic influence in the science fiction trilogy and *The Screwtape Letters*. Our sentinel is no longer with us, but our turn in the great conflict has come and we would do well to heed his warnings.

Chapter 3

Lewis Reaches Out
to His World

"Edmund is my lawful prey!"
Illustration © 2007 by Deborah Wilson Camp

"You have a traitor there, Aslan," said the Witch.

"Well," said Aslan. "His offense was not against you."

"Have you forgotten the Deep Magic?" asked the Witch.

"Let us say I have forgotten it," answered Aslan gravely. "Tell us of this Deep Magic."

"Tell you?" said the Witch ... "You at least know the magic which the Emperor put into Narnia at the very beginning. You know that every traitor belongs to me as my lawful prey and that for every treachery I have a right to a kill."

(LWW: 138–9)

The Witch wanted to claim Edmund for a very good reason: "It's a saying [said Mr. Beaver] in Narnia time out of mind that when two Sons of Adam and two Daughters of Eve sit in those four thrones, then it will be the end not only of the White Witch's reign but of her life" (LWW: 78). If only Edmund could be slain, the prophecy could not come true.

People enjoy *The Chronicles of Narnia* for many reasons, and one of them is the mythology that gives such depth to the story. I have already shown that Lewis's conversion was facilitated by the realization (thanks to J. R. R. Tolkien) that Christianity was the story of a God who actually entered history. Myth became fact. We should hardly be surprised, then, if Lewis wanted to move his readers with the power of myth just as he had been. And the power of myth comes through stories that convey truth. Myth became fact and truth became history. And so, the story of Narnia is the myth, not allegory, telling how Aslan, the creator of Narnia, entered his own creation as a lion, just as Jesus came into his creation as a man.

The Redemption Story: Lewis's Subtle Approach

Telling, or perhaps I should say, retelling the redemption story in various formats reveals its importance to Lewis; indeed, it is the story of stories. Lewis doesn't argue the logic of the gospel in his imaginative works; he appeals to the heart. This is a very effective if subtle approach to evangelism. Later, the mind of the seeker or new believer can benefit from the more logical approach of such books as *Mere Christianity*, but first the heart and the imagination must be captured. The heart of the Christian story is the redemptive work of Christ, and Lewis makes this his focus in *The Lion, The Witch and the Wardrobe, Perelandra*, and *The Great Divorce*. I begin with a brief summary of the final days of Christ's earthly life, death, descent, and resurrection to show how and where Lewis used them in his books.

First, the events leading up to Christ's death. Scholars generally focus upon his last days in Jerusalem, beginning with his entry into that city on a donkey, and concluding with his arrest. The major events in this week would be the last supper with his disciples, and his agony in the garden as he wrestles with God's will. Lewis was deeply moved by God's refusal ("Let this cup pass from me:" Matt 26:39) and abandonment ("Why have you forsaken me?" Matt 27:46) of the one who served him perfectly, and often referred to it in his writings. If the prayer of the sinless Jesus went unanswered, Lewis knew it could be his own experience as well. He cautioned his readers more than once to expect fewer answered prayers as they matured in their faith.

Next, the sufferings and death of Jesus, or his "passion." Jesus was arrested, sent to several different people for hearings before Jewish and Roman officials, and finally condemned on the testimony of false witnesses. Once sentenced to death, he was mocked, stripped, beaten, crowned with thorns, and crucified.

Finally, Lewis is very interested in the events between the death and the resurrection of Jesus. Biblical passages speak of the body of Jesus being placed in a borrowed tomb (Matt 27:59–60), his soul descending into Hades (Acts 2:27), where he took "captivity captive" (Eph 4:7–8), preparing a place for his disciples (John 14:2), being raised from the dead, and returning from Hades and the grave in triumph, and proclaiming: "I have the keys of death and Hades" (Rev 1:18).

The redemption story in _The Lion, the Witch and the Wardrobe_

Lewis began _The Chronicles of Narnia_ with this volume, which was an attempt to form a story around the image of a faun which had been in his mind for many years. But when Aslan the lion abruptly entered his thoughts (Lewis couldn't explain how!), a story did emerge, and the plot soon developed into the retelling of the redemption story adapted to fit the world of Narnia.

The gospels describe Jesus choosing to go up to Jerusalem, knowing the fate that awaited him there. The treachery of Edmund confronts Aslan with the same decision to give up his life. Quite a few things happen there in the last week of the earthly lives of Jesus and Aslan, but both Lewis and the gospels indicate that the White Witch/Satan is especially busy at this time. Jesus tells Peter that Satan wants to sift him and the other disciples "like wheat." But his prayers for Peter will steady him, and when Peter has recovered, he should help the others (Luke 22:31–34). And, of course, Satan has more success with Judas, who betrays Jesus after Satan has entered into him (John 13:27).

Lewis doesn't try to replicate all of these details, but the Witch does ask for an audience with Aslan. Once granted, she reveals her purpose in coming: "You have a traitor there,

Aslan." Aslan responds that Edmund has not wronged her, but the Witch reminds him (Lewis uses the Witch to inform his readers) of the Deep Magic instituted by the Emperor at the very beginning of Narnia. Every traitor becomes the Witch's "lawful prey" (LWW: 138–9). As Christ died for sinful humanity, Aslan will choose to die for Edmund.

In the gospels, Jesus next observes the last supper with his disciples and then goes to the Garden of Gethsemane to pray. Lewis also includes a final supper, but it's not a special meal or a new covenant, nor does he depict Aslan praying, but he does emphasize the sense of impending doom. After the meal, Susan and Lucy are unable to sleep. They decide to get up and check on Aslan, and in the moonlight they see him leaving the camp and walking into the wood. His head and tail are drooping, and he walks as if completely exhausted. When Aslan sees them, he allows them to accompany him and they stroke his mane to comfort him when he tells them he is sad and lonely (LWW: 144–8). Leaving them concealed in the woods, Aslan walks further to the mob awaiting him at the Stone Table. As in the gospel accounts, the women will become witnesses of the suffering and death, though in *The Lion, the Witch and the Wardrobe*, the girls cover their eyes at the moment of Aslan's death.

Here are some of the more obvious parallels between the sufferings of Christ and Aslan (LWW: 149–52):

- A contingent of soldiers comes to the Garden of Gethsemane to arrest Jesus, accompanied by the high priest and other leaders. Jesus rebukes them, but yields, adding: "This is your hour and the power of darkness" (Luke 22:53). Lewis depicts the satanic involvement in Aslan's demise by having the lion seized by a horde of ogres, wraiths, and other monsters.
- The chief priests and the elders bind Jesus when they have decided his guilt and send him to Pilate (Matt 27:2). The

White Witch orders Aslan bound, and four hags set upon him, soon aided by evil dwarfs and apes. They roll him over on his back and tie his paws together. After much abuse, he is bound again, this time to the stone table.

- Next, the Witch decides Aslan should be shaved. The gospels do not mention Jesus being shaved, but Lewis includes this to reflect Isa 50:6, a prophetic passage foretelling the treatment of the Messiah: "I gave my back to those who struck me, and my cheeks to those who pulled out the beard; I did not hide my face from insult and spitting."

- Aslan doesn't look so fierce after he has been shaved, and the crowd mocks him, calling him Puss and asking how many mice he's caught or if he'd like a saucer of milk. The greatness of Jesus is also derided. The soldiers put a purple robe on him, a crown of thorns, place a reed in his hand for a scepter, and kneel before him in pretend worship (Matt 27:27–30).

- Jesus remains silent before Pilate (Matt 27:11–14); Aslan offers no resistance, neither moving nor roaring, but is muzzled anyway.

- Jesus is struck when the high priest accuses him of blasphemy (Matt 26:64–68), and later by the soldiers, who also spit upon him (Matt 27:30). Both Jesus and Aslan remain silent. After Aslan has been muzzled, the crowd attacks, kicking, hitting, and spitting upon him.

- Aslan is tied to the stone table, and Jesus is nailed to the cross (Matt 27:35).

- The Witch dispatches Aslan with a strangely shaped stone knife; a soldier pierces the side of Jesus with his sword (John 19:34). Blood and water come from Jesus's side; blood and foam from Aslan.

As in the gospels, no human actually witnesses the resurrection, since Jesus is sealed in a tomb with Roman guards posted to prevent anyone from entering. In *The Lion, the Witch and the Wardrobe*, the event also goes unnoticed, since the girls are walking around to ward off the cold. (A wise decision on the part of Lewis; how does one describe a resurrection?) But in preparation for Aslan's return to life, mice gnaw through the ropes that bind him, a fitting touch for an animal world, and perhaps inspired by a Roman historian. In the essay "Miracles" Lewis observed that angels stopped Sennacherib's invasion of Israel (2 Chron 32:21), while Herodotus wrote that many mice came and chewed through his army's bowstrings ("God in the Dock" in GID: 28).

Just as the sun appears, the girls hear a loud cracking noise, as if "a giant had broken a giant's plate" (LWW: 158). Returning to the stone table, they find it broken in half, and empty. They burst into tears. In the gospels, Luke describes the women who come at dawn to anoint the body with spices as perplexed at the empty tomb (Luke 24:1–4), but in John's account, Mary weeps because she believes that the body of Jesus has been removed. Turning around she discovers Jesus standing there. Likewise, Lucy and Susan hear a voice behind them and turn to discover Aslan, alive and looking larger than ever. As did the disciples, they wonder if they are seeing a ghost (Luke 24:37; LWW: 159), and in both cases, Jesus/Aslan convinces them that he is real. Jesus invites his disciples to touch him (Luke 24:39); Aslan licks Susan's forehead.

The mysterious stone table requires a separate note. Paul Ford describes it well in his *Companion to Narnia*: it's covered with strange carvings, seems to have been around forever, and its history is unknown. But what does it represent? Since the main point of the Deep Magic is that the Witch has a right to the life of every traitor, and since the stone table is the place where such are killed, one possible interpretation is that the place represents the Old Testament Law, which Paul describes by the words "the ministry of death, chiseled in letters on stone tablets" (2 Cor 3:7). That Law was unforgiving; every sin must be atoned for with blood. But when Christ died in our place, he paid that penalty with his own blood, "erasing the record that stood against us with its legal demands" (Col 2:13). Thus, when Aslan dies, the great stone table is broken in two, signifying that the power of what is written upon it has been nullified, since its demands have been met. The Witch understood the Law. But she did not realize, Aslan says, "that when a willing victim who had committed no treachery was killed in a traitor's stead, the table would crack and Death itself would start working backwards" (LWW: 160).

Sure enough, when Susan and Lucy hear the stone table crack, they rush back to it to find a great crack running down through it. In the gospel account, the veil of the Temple in Jerusalem where sacrifices for sin were offered according to the law was also "cracked;" that is, torn in two from top to bottom (Luke 23:45). But they soon forget the sound because something much worse meets their eyes; Aslan is gone! "Oh, it's *too* bad," sobbed Lucy; "they might have left the body alone." Lucy's tears recall those of Mary Magdalene's, who tells the two angels she weeps because "They have taken away my Lord and I do not know where they have laid him" (John 20:13). In both accounts, the girls, and Mary, then turn around and find Jesus standing there. Susan begins to ask if he is a ghost; Aslan licks her forehead to show he is indeed physically there. The disciples also become frightened when Jesus appears to them, supposing he is a ghost, and he reassures them by inviting them to touch him, and finally, seeing they were still unconvinced, by eating some fish (Luke 24:37–43).

After Aslan comes back to life, he romps with the girls (a passage quite unique to Christian literature) and then flies to the Witch's castle with them on his back. There in the court-yard they find the many animals the Witch had turned to stone, but Aslan returns them to life after breathing on them.

> For a second after Aslan had breathed upon him the stone lion
> looked just the same. Then a tiny streak of gold began to run
> along his white marble back – then it spread – then the colour
> seemed to lick all over him as the flame licks all over a bit of
> paper – then, while his hind-quarters were still obviously stone
> the lion shook his mane and all the heavy, stony folds rippled
> into living hair... everywhere the statues were coming to life.
> The courtyard looked no longer like a museum; it looked more
> like a zoo. (LWW: 165–6)

After finishing with the courtyard, "Now for the inside of this
house!" said Aslan. "Look alive, everyone. Up stairs and down
stairs and in my lady's chamber! Leave no corner unsearched.
You never know where some poor prisoner may be concealed"
(LWW: 167). And so Narnia's "Hades" was winnowed.

The ransacking of the Witch's castle may well be the Narnian version of Christ's descent into the underworld (perhaps
Lewis also had the resurrection of bodies in mind) where he
"took captivity captive" (Eph 4:8). The description of the
Witch's stronghold as a castle also brings to mind Luke
11:21–22, where Jesus is defending himself against the accus-
ation of the Pharisees that he has been using the power of
Beelzebul (Satan) to cast out demons. The correct understanding of his ministry is that Jesus opposes Satan and has nothing
to do with his power. Jesus depicts his ministry by this metaphor: the castle of a strong man has been invaded by an even
stronger man, who overpowers the owner and then takes
whatever he wishes from the castle. So then, both the earthly
ministry of Jesus and his descent into Hades (the dungeon of
the castle!) represent the plundering of Satan's possessions.

But since Aslan had flown over the wall, they were all still
trapped in the courtyard, as the gates were still locked. At
the request of Aslan, Giant Rumblebuffin smashes the gates
with his club, and then the towers on each side (LWW: 169).
This again reflects Biblical imagery, such as Isaiah 38:10:

"I said: In the noontide of my days I must depart; I am consigned to the *gates of Sheol* for the rest of my years," and Matthew 16:18: "And I tell you, you are Peter, and on this rock I will build my church, and the *gates of Hades* will not prevail against it." Christ has changed what the Old Testament saints knew as a permanent prison into a temporary place for souls.

Lewis concludes the redemption story in *The Lion, the Witch and the Wardrobe* with a post-resurrection appearance of Aslan, again following the lead of the gospels. In the gospel of John, Jesus appears to several of his disciples when they are fishing at the Sea of Tiberias. When they recognize Jesus and have caught many fish by following his instructions, they come to shore and find waiting a charcoal fire with fish and bread. John does not tell us the source of this food. Likewise, at the last meeting between Aslan and the children, they have a meal together. "How Aslan provided food for them all I don't know; but somehow or other they found themselves all sitting down on the grass to a fine high tea at about eight o'clock" (LWW: 178).

And after that? "These two Kings and two Queens governed Narnia well and long and happy was their reign" (LWW: 180). This too is Biblical, for the ultimate destiny of the redeemed is to rule with Christ when he returns (Rev 20:4).

The Lion, the Witch and the Wardrobe now can be seen as the Christian story in an imaginary world. It resembles the ancient myths because the ancient myths foretold Christianity. The essential plot is a human fall that destroys an ideal life between humans and the gods. Then a divine figure appears, dies, and comes back to life to restore harmony. Only one person "falls" in Narnia, but his betrayal brings him under the control of the Witch who prepares to prevent the fulfillment of the prophecy. All of Narnia will be under her control forever if she succeeds.

As the above comparison shows, Lewis may have taken his liberty in adapting the gospel narratives for his own Narnian purposes, but he still reflects them to a remarkable degree. He obviously knew the Biblical traditions well, believed them to constitute the greatest story of all, and was confident the power of the story would remain effective in a variety of fictional settings.

Next, the redemptive work of Christ as reflected in *Perelandra*.

The redemption story in *Perelandra*

Perelandra is the second volume of the space trilogy; *Out of the Silent Planet* is the first and *That Hideous Strength* is the third. In volume one, Ransom is kidnapped and taken to Mars, an old planet. But in *Perelandra*, a good angel sends him to Venus, a new planet with only two people on it. "Suppose . . . in some other planet there were a first couple undergoing the same that Adam and Eve underwent here, but successfully" ("To Mrs. Hook" in L: 475, December 29, 1958). The conflict begins when Weston arrives from earth and becomes possessed by Satan. Through Weston, Satan attempts to persuade Tinidril, the first woman of her planet, to disobey the single command for her planet, just as he tempted Eve in the Garden of Eden. Ransom does his best to help the woman resist the temptations, but Weston won't stop. Finally, Ransom realizes the only option left is to physically attack Weston, and the battle is joined. Once again, the fate of an entire world hangs in the balance.

Ransom's destiny

Although *Perelandra* lacks many of the specific details of Christ's suffering that Lewis included in *The Lion, the Witch and the Wardrobe*, the contents of the gospels are prominent once more. Lewis picks up the gospel thread with his version of Jesus in the Garden of Gethsemane. The gospels describe Jesus in agonized prayer as he reflects upon what awaits him in Jerusalem, while his disciples unsuccessfully try to stay awake (Matt 26:36–46). In *Perelandra*, Ransom has no one to pray with him, but at least his opponent, the Unman (Weston possessed by Satan), has been cast into sleep by Maledil (God). Indeed, even the Lady and the animals in the vicinity have all been put asleep so that their innocence will not be marred by the physical violence that will soon ensue.

And so, all through chapter eleven, Ransom struggles to grasp his situation and to discover what God wants him to do. I realized only a few years ago that all of this chapter is set in the total darkness that characterizes Perelandrian night. In the fourth gospel, after Satan enters into Judas and he leaves the last supper to betray Jesus, John adds these ominous words: "And it was night" (John 13:30).

In *Perelandra*, the three prayers of Jesus in the garden are expanded into a conversation with God, though Ransom does most of the talking. Lewis depicts the intensity of the struggle by having Ransom groan, writhe, and even grind his teeth. Three times God says to him "This can't go on," meaning the relentless tempting of the Lady by the Unman; that is, Weston now possessed by Satan. God's will for Ransom also proves to be threefold. Ransom must accept that he is God's instrument, that he must act and not just wait in faith for God to do something, and that he has been brought to Perelandra to engage the Unman in a physical battle – a daunting prospect for an out-of-shape professor!

A less obvious parallel between Christ and Ransom revolves around their persons and not just their actions. Jesus is "the Lamb slain before the foundation of the world" (1 Pet 1:19–20), and Ransom learns during the night that he also has been predestined for the conflict that will help determine the fate of Venus.

> He knew now why the old philosophers had said that there is
> no such thing as chance or fortune beyond the Moon. Before
> his Mother had born him, before his ancestors had been called
> Ransoms, before *ransom* had been the name for a payment that
> delivers, before the world was made, all these things had so
> stood together in eternity that the very significance of the
> pattern at this point lay in their coming together in just this
> fashion. (PER: 125)

Ransom's only comfort comes in the fact that God identified
with him, saying: "My name is also Ransom" (PER: 126). If
he should fail, God would still, somehow, provide another
solution, another ransom. But it will cost him even more
than on earth, and Ransom finally realizes that he is the
chosen one, and yet has freedom to choose to fight the
Unman. Predestination and free will no longer seem different,
and he chooses to obey.

The battle

Once the Unman realizes that Ransom intends to fight him, he
does the unexpected. With a loud voice he cries out: "Eloi,
Eloi, lama sabachthani" (PER: 130). Satan has remembered
these Aramaic words of Jesus (Mark 15:34) and now he uses
them to torment Ransom. Jesus died alone and forsaken, and
Ransom can expect the same fate.

The battle itself is ferocious, with neither yielding an inch.
The Unman leaps upon Ransom and those same, long, sharp
fingernails that tortured the frog-like creatures not long before
now tear strips of skin and flesh from Ransom's back. This
recalls the multi-thong *flagellum* which the Romans generally
used to whip criminals before crucifixion. Jesus suffered in this
manner at the command of Pilate (Mark 15:15).

Eventually, the ferocity of Ransom's attack forces the
Unman to flee. Ransom pursues but is unable to overtake

him. After a long chase, Weston takes to the ocean riding on the back of a porpoise-like fish, with Ransom still following on another fish. During the hours' long chase, he realizes that he is very thirsty. But after trying for half an hour to bend over and get a drink, the stiffness of his battered body prevents him from managing more than a tiny sip "which merely mocked his thirst." Jesus likewise became thirsty, but was mocked by being offered only some vinegar on a sponge (John 19:28).

Finally, when both fish become weary, Ransom does catch up to Weston, who seems to have come back to himself. But after a discussion of life and death, Weston suddenly grabs him and pulls him down into the water. Just when Ransom thinks he must surely die, they emerge into an underground cavern and the battle continues. In the gospels, Jesus dies on the cross, but in *Perelandra* the struggle does not lead to Ransom's death, for he is only a mortal and resurrection is not an option. But Ransom does experience a symbolic death. His descent in the clutches of the Unman to the underground cavern is Lewis's version of Christ being "in the heart of the earth" (Matt 12:39); that is, Hades, after his death. Thanks to Lewis, we can imagine Satan waiting for Jesus to breathe his last on the cross and then pulling his soul down to the underworld, hoping for a victorious conclusion to the struggle there.

As the struggle continues underground, Ransom chokes the Unman until he seems lifeless. Yet even then Satan once again uses Weston's body to continue the pursuit. Finally, after a brief, Trinitarian prayer ("In the name of the Father and of the Son and of the Holy Ghost, here goes – I mean Amen," PER: 155), Ransom smashes the Unman's head with a stone and pushes the body over a cliff. It falls into a sea of fire far below, and the battle is finally over. The way the struggle ends clearly recalls Genesis 3:15, where God tells the serpent that someday one of Eve's descendants will crush his head. (The church fathers referred to this passage as the *protoeuangelion*, the

Greek word for "first gospel," because it is the earliest promise of Christ's redemption in the Bible.) And the fiery pit recalls the lake of fire reserved for Satan and his angels (Matt 25:41). Finally, Lewis based his description of this pit as "a terrible place where clouds of steam went up for ever and ever" (PER: 183) on Revelation 19:20 and 20:10, where the smoke ascends forever from the lake of fire.

After Christ's descent into Hades, he ascended; first to the earth where he appeared to many and gave further instructions to his disciples, and then to Heaven where he took his place at the right side of his Father. Ransom's ascent also has two parts. After a long, painful climb he finally falls into an underground river which brings him back to the surface and deposits him into a shallow pool. Crawling out of the warm water he rests on the soft turf, eating nearby fruit until his battered body is healed many days later. When he is nearly well, he notices for the first time that his heel has a wound (from a bite – the Unman was a dirty fighter!) that refuses to heal. This is Lewis's version of Christ who retained the scars of his death by crucifixion even in his resurrection body. Like Jesus, Ransom bears in his "resurrection" body the evidence of his suffering. The injured heel also represents the other half of the prediction of Genesis 3:15: "you [the serpent] will strike his heel."

The second part of Ransom's "post-resurrection" experiences brings him not into Heaven but climbing to the highest point on the planet, where he walks on rose-colored (Easter?) lilies. There, for the first time, his bleeding heel leaves no trace. Then, at a sacred place in a valley, Ransom speaks with the Adam and Eve of Perelandra, next with the angelic rulers of Mars and Venus, and finally he experiences a beatific vision. Then he does indeed ascend into the Heavens, but this journey returns him to his own planet.

Looking back, we can see that Lewis wanted to tell the redemption story in novel form, knowing the power of this greatest of all stories. And the essential parts are all present, from the agony in the garden to the suffering, the descent into the "lower parts of the earth," and finally the resurrection and ascent into Heavenly places.

The fondness of Lewis for the redemption story of the gospels and his willingness to modify it within the new context of Narnia, also holds true in the Ransom trilogy. For example, the Aramaic cry of despair now comes from Satan, not the one who is about to die. Also, Ransom doesn't literally die, as did Jesus, nor does he descend to Hades, or ascend into Heaven. And yet the basic pattern remains. Ransom struggles with the will of God; next he suffers a symbolic death, triumphs over his enemy in the underworld, and ascends from the heart of the planet to its highest point, where he experiences a beatific vision.

Note the reluctance of Lewis to repeat himself when describing the smaller details. Virtually none of the ways in which Aslan suffered are repeated here. Nor does Aslan experience the specific details of Ransom's conflict. For example, the cry of Aramaic is missing in *The Lion, the Witch and the Wardrobe*, nor is Aslan whipped, though this is a prominent feature of Christ's abuse in the gospels. But Ransom has his back torn by the Unman's fingernails. If we combine the two accounts, nearly everything in the gospels is accounted for, excluding the various trials that Jesus went through before Jewish and Roman authorities – events that specifically apply only to first-century Palestine.

The myth that entered history

What effect would these stories of Aslan's death and Ransom's struggle have on readers who were not familiar with the Bible and perhaps even hostile to organized religion? The power of this approach is that it is, one might say, pre-religious. The pattern of a stronger person, perhaps even a divine person, sacrificing himself for a weaker person appeals to the human heart, since we are touched by examples of fortitude motivated by love. Now, should the reader of Lewis encounter the gospel story, the redemptive work of Christ will have a familiar ring to it and will resonate with the same deep appeal that Narnia brings.

Such is the strategy of the "dinosaur" who knew that his kind was nearly extinct. The study of the classics (the writings of "dead white men") he enjoyed was disappearing; few modern readers know the old myths. So in *The Lion, the Witch and the Wardrobe* and in *Perelandra*, Lewis wrote his own versions of them, based on the gospel accounts as we have seen. They are not allegories but myths. They convey the pattern of truth as they describe the God acting on behalf of his creation.

The significance of this can hardly be overstated. When Lewis perceived that the incarnation, life, death, and resurrection of Jesus were myth become history, he realized that the older myths told much the same story, though often distorted. "The truth first appears in *mythical* form and then by a long process of condensing or focusing finally becomes incarnate as History" (M: 139, footnote 1). That they shared the same themes was no accident; for Lewis, they were "good dreams . . . scattered all through the heathen religions about a god who dies and comes to life again and, by his death, has somehow given new life to men" (MC: 39). One might say Christianity has "redeemed" the old myths that Lewis once described as "breathing a lie through silver" ("On Fairy Stories" in *Essays Presented to Charles Williams*: 71). Now we see them for what they actually were: God-given stories about God that were given to prepare pre-Christian cultures for the truest story of all.

In effect, Lewis is also saying this is the story of stories. There are many religions and beliefs in the world, and most of them share elements of the Christian story. Lewis did not find this surprising, nor a threat to Christianity, since humans every-where share the values of the Tao. But only in Israel, only once in our history, and only in Jesus did God enter time and space in human flesh. "The Hebrews, like other peoples, had mythology: but as they were the chosen people so their myth-ology was the chosen mythology – the mythology chosen by God to be the vehicle of the earliest sacred truths, the first step in that process which ends in the New Testament where truth has become completely historical" (M: 139, footnote 1). As Jesus told the woman of Samaria he witnessed to at the well, "salvation is of the Jews" (John 4:22).

In the story of stories, Lewis believed, God has revealed the only way for sinful humanity to find redemption. As God's storyteller, Lewis reached out to the imagination of his readers. But as a theologian, if only an amateur, he knew quite well the implications of the faith. If Jesus is indeed "the way, the truth, and the life" as he claimed (John 14:6), what of the untold billions who have lived and died without hearing the story? Must they all be lost? Lewis found the answer, in the Scriptures as we might expect, and the solution is nearly as incredible as the story itself. In fact, it is part of the story and we shall return to this problem and its solution in chapter six.

The Redemption Story: Lewis's Direct Approach

In chapter two, I introduced the "quarrel approach" Lewis used to convince his wartime listeners that there was a moral law that people of all times and cultures could largely agree on. Returning to those radio talks as they now stand in *Mere Christianity*, we discover there is a logical progression from that starting point to a relationship with God. But the path was not easy for Lewis, since his countrymen had little or no sense of conviction in their lives. How then could he convince them of their need for salvation?

Since we cannot "see" God anywhere in the universe, Lewis decided to place his focus upon humanity. Would there be any evidence for God in ourselves? The answer for Lewis is "yes;" God can show himself to us "as an influence or a command trying to get us to behave in a certain way" (MC: 19). It logically follows then that the moral law reflects its source. Someone is very interested in right conduct, and even when bravery or honesty or faithfulness to one's spouse is difficult or dangerous, that law within continues to insist on the straight thing. Since humans often fail to do the right thing, the source of that law must hate much of what we do, or fail to do. We are at odds with our Creator, and in danger of condemnation.

Now that Lewis has brought his readers to the realization of a personal God who is attempting to guide them into right behavior, and has confronted them with the fact that they often fail, he can progress to the solution of this problem. And of course, that's where Christ and Christianity come in. But first Lewis anticipates a thoughtful person asking how the world came to be such a mess. It certainly doesn't reflect in all its wars, cruelty, and suffering the kind of place the author of the moral law would create or desire.

Christianity comes to the rescue with the explanation Lewis prefers. The world has become a dangerous place because an evil being has made it so. The only other alternative is dualism: the belief that two equal but opposite beings are engaged in an eternal struggle for control. Lewis quickly dismisses this possibility by pointing out that an evil being cannot be the equal of God, the good being. If the evil being has any kind of plan or strategy for success, achievement is possible only by the use of intelligence and the force of will. But these are positive attributes in and of themselves; evil uses them for twisted purposes. Evil, then, is only good gone bad; a parasite in the end. And that is the answer Christianity provides. A powerful angel has decided to rebel against God, and other angels (but by no means all of them) have decided to join his cause. The goal of Satan is to frustrate God's purposes in this world and since God's purposes are focused upon us, we have become his targets.

Chapter two set forth Lewis's belief that Satan's influence in our world must be taken into account if we are to understand the course of history. Lewis is to be commended for his honesty. He did not disguise the fact that any one who accepts his invitation to embrace Christianity will find himself entering enemy-occupied territory. "Christianity is the story of how the rightful king has landed, you might say landed in disguise, and is calling us all to take part in a great campaign of sabotage. When you go to church you are really listening-in to the secret wireless from our friends: that is why the enemy is so anxious to prevent us from going" (MC: 36).

Into this world gone bad comes God's answer. For centuries God worked with the Jews to reveal to them what he was like, and then "there suddenly turns up a man who goes about talking as if He was God. He claims to forgive sins. He says He has always existed. He says He is coming to judge the world at the end of time" (MC: 40). Lewis especially wanted his audience to grasp the significance of Jesus forgiving sins. "This makes sense only if He really was the God whose laws are broken and whose love is wounded in every sin. In the mouth of any other speaker who is not God, these words would imply what I can only regard as a silliness and conceit unrivalled by any other character in history" (MC: 40).

With these dramatic words, Lewis reaches the point of decision. Either Jesus is a lunatic or he is the Son of God. But there is no other choice; no middle ground. Regular, sane people do not make such claims and predictions. Even to acclaim him as a great moral teacher, a prophet, or a compassionate leader is to sell him short. Madman or God-man are the only two possibilities.

God's Life in Us

So why did God send his Son into the world? Lewis answers this question in two ways. The first way looks back in time. On the cross, Jesus atoned for our sins. There are several views of the atonement – oddly enough, Christians have never been able to agree on which is best – but Lewis prefers the interpretation that Christ died to pay a debt that we are unable to pay. The second way looks to the future: what does God intend to accomplish in our lives after forgiving our sins? What does he want from us?

There is no compromise in Lewis's answer: God wants every part of us. He demands perfection, and will never stop (unless we resist him) until we are perfect. "This is the whole of Christianity. There is nothing else ... the Church exists for nothing else but to draw men into Christ, to make them little Christs" (MC: 155).

Many people find this difficult to accept because they assume that only God is perfect. But Lewis reminds us that God's plan for us includes more than just forgiveness of sins, though that is certainly a wonderful gift. Christ not only gave his life *for* us, he intends to give his life *to* us as well. We have by birth, Lewis points out, *Bios* life – the Greek word for "natural life." God wants to give us spiritual or *Zoe* life – the kind of life he has (MC: 123). In other words, we need more than improvement; we need to be born again. We won't become God, but we will become perfect humans.

It won't be easy; the natural *Bios* life is self-centered and used to being in charge. Christ will expose it for what it is,

Lewis promises, if we allow him to. Jesus is, after all, "a living Man, still as much a man as you, and still as much God as He was when He created the world, really coming and interfering with your very self; killing the old natural self in you and replacing it with the kind of self He has" (MC: 149). We become moral creatures in three ways as this new life is formed in us. God cleans us up inside, he helps us achieve fair play and harmony with others, and finally puts us on the right path in life: "the general purpose of human life as a whole" (MC: 57). Just what we are as humans, and what we are designed to do in this world, will be the subject of the next chapter.

The implication of what Lewis is saying is there is no hope for us outside of Christ, because he is the only perfect One who died for our sins and who has the divine life we need. The natural *Bios* life will never produce spiritual life. This clears up what seems to be a problem in Genesis, where God told our first parents not to eat of the tree of the knowledge of good and evil. If they did, they would die that very day, and yet Adam went on to live more than 900 years. But only Adam's (and Eve's) natural life remained; the spiritual life was gone and the same is true of all their descendants.

This need to be born from above is a central truth in redemption. Lewis did well to emphasize it, for there are two ancient and very popular misconceptions about it that have survived until today. The first "theology" would agree: we must be born again, and we will – many, many times until we finally reach a state of nothingness and become "one" with the universe. Millions upon millions of people in the East have accepted this view, and reincarnation has even made inroads into Christianity itself. But reincarnation offers nothing but a series of existences meant to gradually improve the natural life. Improvement is not the answer, Lewis reminds us; only Christ's spiritual life will do.

The other view also tries to get as close to the truth as possible, and comes to us with optimism in its face. We have been created in God's image, but most of us have forgotten or have never been told. And so we live much as animals, letting the natural life rule us. What we need to know, and knowledge is the key here, is that there is still a spark (others prefer the metaphor of a seed) of divine life within. Once we begin to conduct ourselves in that realization and subdue the physical part of ourselves with its appetites, we will realize that the goal of our existence is to ultimately escape the physical world and become spirit beings.

This view comes in many shapes and disguises, but they all belong to the philosophy known as Gnosticism. Matter is sinful and our bodies are a prison from which death will release us. Since many of the early Christian leaders came from a background filled with influences from Greek philosophy, Gnosticism soon became prominent in the church. By the fourth century of the Christian era it would not be inaccurate to say that there were two major "versions" of Christianity. Gnosticism eventually was rejected as unorthodox, but not before many were led to deny the humanity of Christ (why would God contaminate himself with matter?), celibacy became required of every priest, and original sin became defined as sex between Adam and Eve, rather than disobedience. Gnosticism, in one form or another, may well be the most popular and widespread belief system in the history of the world, and Lewis thoroughly discredited it when he depicted the attempts of NICE to achieve immortality by escape from the body.

Returning to the life found only in Christ, it would appear that Lewis has painted himself into a theological corner. Ancient mythologies prepared their cultures for the time when God entered history, died, and rose again. As God incarnate, he is the only One who can atone for sin if we believe in him.

And he wants to purify us – to sanctify us – by giving us his life to gradually replace our natural life. But what does this mean for all of those who lived and died before Christ, or who have lived in cultures not yet reached with the message?

There would seem to be no hope. Even if someone did manage to lead a very good life, effort spent in serving and loving others, while commendable, does not bring us divine life. That comes only from a divine source. Untold billions must be lost. But, Lewis reminds us, we must not look at this situation from our perspective, limited as it is to time and space. We experience time as past, present, and future, and actually can act within it only "now" – in the present time which will soon become past. But God is not so limited. All of time is "now" for him. He has forever to listen to each of our prayers and to watch each of us act. Judas did not betray Jesus because his act of treachery was predicted in the Psalms and so he had no choice but to fulfill prophecy. Lewis would say that God saw Judas freely choose (under the influence of Satan, the gospels tell us) to lead the priests and soldiers to Jesus in the Garden of Gethsemane. And because Judas made that choice, and because God is not limited by time as we are, he was free to inspire David to compose a prophetic song about what would occur a thousand years later.

Looking at humanity from God's perspective outside of time, or also from within all of time at once, the human race would not appear to God as a lot of individual people, but as a very complicated family tree showing every human connected to every other human. And when Christ becomes man and enters history, "the effect spreads through all mankind. It makes a difference to people who lived before Christ as well as people who lived after Him. It makes a difference to people who have never heard of Him" (MC: 141). God is not limited by time or space, and neither is his salvation. But when, where, and how did God accomplish not only redemption for everyone who has ever lived and ever will live, but also his plan for perfecting us? The theology Lewis formed to answer these questions will be the subject of chapter six.

Before then, Lewis has something to say about humanity. We do not live alone on this planet; mankind is part of the created order of things. Lewis saw our place as just above the animals and just below angels, and also as having much in common with both groups. Only when mankind becomes reconciled with God's help to the animal life within and also what we share with angels will the third goal of morality be realized: the general purpose of human life.

Chapter 4

Humanity in God's Creation

"By the touch and breath of Aslan, Narnia is born."
Illustration © 2007 by Deborah Wilson Camp

And now, for the first time, the Lion was silent. He was going to and fro among the animals. And every now and then he would go up to two of them (always two at a time) and touch their noses with his ... The pairs which he had touched instantly left their own kinds and followed him ... The Lion, whose eyes never blinked, stared at the animals as hard as if he was going to burn them up with his mere stare. And gradually a change came over them ... the Lion opened his mouth, but no sound came from it; he was breathing out, a long, warm breath; it seemed to sway all the beasts as the wind sways a line of trees ... Then there came a swift flash like fire (but it burnt nobody) either from the sky or from the Lion itself, and every drop of blood tingled in the children's bodies, and the deepest, wildest voice they had ever heard was saying: "Narnia, Narnia, Narnia, awake. Love. Think. Speak. Be walking trees. Be talking beasts. Be divine waters."

(MN: 115–16)

And so Narnia was born. What about our planet?

The Making of Humanity

By the time Lewis became a Christian and began to study the Scriptures, Darwin's views on the origin and development of life were having a profound influence upon science and the church alike. In addition to evolution, different branches of science such as archaeology, geology, and astronomy were also challenging the Biblical account of six literal days of creation some six thousand years ago. The universe, and our world, seemed much more ancient than that; billions of years older.

Lewis, of course, was aware of these developments and seems to have accepted the claims of science for the great age of the universe. On the other hand, he did not relinquish the Biblical description of humans as more than just animals.

At some point, he believed, God selected an anthropoid and breathed into him his life so that he became fully human. (See, for example, his letter to Sister Penelope in L: 417, January 10, 1952.) This view is one version of theistic evolution and by it Lewis was able to accept the evidence for the gradual development of life on earth over millennia without ruling out divine miracles to guide that development.

These selected humans were more than just beasts, they had a new responsibility that came with this new life.

> "Creatures, I give you yourselves," said the strong, happy voice of Aslan. "I give to you forever this land of Narnia. I give you the woods, the fruits, the rivers. I give you the stars and I give you myself. The Dumb Beasts whom I have not chosen are yours also. Treat them gently and cherish them but do not go back to their ways lest you cease to be Talking Beasts. For out of them you were taken and into them you can return. Do not so." (MN: 118)

But, sadly, humanity in this world did return.

> For long centuries God perfected the animal form which was to become the vehicle of humanity and the image of himself... Then, in the fullness of time, God caused to descend upon this organism, both on its psychology and physiology, a new kind of consciousness which could say "I" and "me," which knew God, which could make judgements [*sic*] of truth, beauty, and goodness, and which was so far above time that it could perceive time flowing past... Wholly commanding himself, he commanded all lower lives with which he came into contact. Even now we meet rare individuals who have a mysterious power of taming beasts... We do not know how many of these creatures God made, nor how long they continued in the Paradisal state. But sooner or later they fell. Someone or something whispered that they could become as gods... They wanted some corner in the universe of which they could say to

God, "This is our business, not yours." But there is no such corner. (PP: 77–80)

The result of the fall was discord.

> The natural self since the Fall consists of body, soul, and spirit all perverted & self centred and at odds with one another. Animalness (the body & what arises from it) is not in itself bad: what is bad is the rebellious *relation* in wh. it now stands to the other parts. But its rebellion against spirit is less terrible than spirit's rebellion against God. ("Letter to Mr. Lyell" in CL II: 632; December 6, 1944)

This discord now affects everyone, because "a new species, never made by God, had sinned itself into existence." In a rather poetic manner, Lewis describes God's response to the fall of man: "The world is a dance in which good, descending from God, is disturbed by evil arising from the creatures, and the resulting conflict is resolved by God's own assumption of the suffering nature which evil produces" (PP: 83–4).

Many conservative Christians do not accept Lewis's view of human evolution, but I am certain he would prefer to stress what they have in common with him: humanity has fallen and no amount of effort from us will change our sinful nature. As Lewis stressed in *Mere Christianity*, the only hope we have begins with the incarnation ("God's own assumption of the suffering nature"), then the atonement, and ends by being transformed by the divine nature offered us in Christ.

Lewis is certainly Biblical in his description of the strained relations between our body and soul and between us and God as a result of original sin. But he doesn't stop there. The discord also now exists between us and the physical world. Everything has been affected; what is above us (God and angels), what is on our level (others) and even the parts of ourselves, and what is below us in the created order. Yet, in our fallen condition, though relations between humans and nature are strained, they still exist. To be in a body means we are part of the physical world and still have been appointed to care for this planet. Let's take a closer look at what we are in relation to creation.

Lewis had a healthy, balanced approach to the body, even though his own was too clumsy for any sport but swimming.

> I have a kindly feeling for the old rattle-trap. Through it God showed me that whole side of His beauty which is embodied in colour, sound, smell and size. No doubt it has often led me astray: but not half so often, I suspect, as my soul has led *it* astray. For the spiritual evils which we share with the devils (pride, spite) are far worse than what we share with the beasts: and sensuality really arises more from the imagination than from the appetites; which, if left merely to their own animal strength, and not elaborated by our imagination, would be fairly easily managed. (LAL: 108; November 26, 1962)

This letter describes well the advantages, and dangers, that arise from sharing the natures of both animals and angels. Lewis feels no shame from having a body; God made us that way. Lewis gives humanity's twofold nature a humorous twist when he has Screwtape call his human patient an amphibian! "As spirits they belong to the eternal world, but as animals they inhabit time. This means that while their spirit can be directed to an eternal object, their bodies, passions, and imaginations are in continual change, for to be in time means to change" (SL: 36–7). Let's consider first our relationship to animals.

Humans and Animals

Most people think of English literature or children's stories or books and articles that encourage Christians when they pay tribute to Lewis, but there is another side to Lewis as well. He thought and wrote so much about animals that any discussion of his theology must include this subject, and it's about time, for animals are probably the most neglected subject in the current discussion of Lewis. (The same could be said of Christian theology in general.) Janine Goffar's very helpful index of subjects in Lewis's theological works provides a rough estimate of the importance of animals for Lewis. She lists seventeen entries for angels, but fifty-five for animals, not counting other entries for cats, creatures, dogs, and pets! (*C. S. Lewis Index*: 29–33).

To begin with, Lewis loved animals.

> Such natural love twixt beast and man we find
> That children all desire an animal book.
> ("Eden's Courtesy" in P: 98)

If the pain and suffering humans experience concerned him, the pains of animals presented him with an even greater theological problem. Taking into account original sin, humans in a sense deserve the consequences of disobedience. The important thing for Lewis about pain is that God can use trials for good purposes. "I assume that the process of purification will normally involve suffering. Partly from tradition; partly because most real good that has been done me in this life has involved it" (LTM: 109).

But the same is not true of animals. They neither deserve pain, nor are they helped by it.

> The animal creation is a strange mystery. We can make some attempt to understand human suffering: but the sufferings of animals from the beginning of the world until now (inflicted not only by us but by one another) – what is one to think? And again, how strange that God brings us into such intimate relations with creatures of whose real purpose and destiny we remain forever ignorant. (LAL: 106, October 26, 1962)

And again: "We know neither what they are nor why they are" ("The Pains of Animals" in GID: 167).

Lewis found it difficult to reconcile undeserved animal pain with the original creation that God pronounced "very, very good" (Gen 1:31). He ventured that since animals existed before us (a nod to evolution or at least the great age of the earth), and since sin began with the angels, the creation may have been affected by fallen angels before humans existed. In their corrupted state, many animals now survive by eating other animals, while God's original plan for them was to eat plants. Lewis based this view on Genesis 1:29, where God tells Adam and Eve that he has given them plants to eat; and Genesis 1:30, where birds and land animals are also given all plants to eat. That some plants eat other plants is not sinful, since they are already given to animals and humans for food.

> The Satanic corruption of the beasts would therefore be analo-
> gous, in one respect, to the Satanic corruption of man. For one
> result of man's fall was that his animality fell back from the
> humanity into which it had been taken up but which could no
> longer rule it. In the same way, animality may have been
> encouraged to slip back into behaviour proper to vegetables.
> (PP: 135)

Since Adam and Eve were given dominion and responsibility for this planet, it follows that we, their offspring, can also
"lift up" or "pull down" our environment. The land must still
be farmed, though thorns will grow more readily than food
plants (Gen 3:17–18). Lewis insists mankind must strive to
relate to animals and treat them well; they are an essential
part of the environment and we need them for many reasons.
Sin, whether from the fall of Satan or man, or both, has
created a rift between us and them so that they now fear us
(Gen 9:2), but the gap can with effort be bridged. The potential
to do them good or evil still exists. The task of managing the

earth will be more difficult now that sin has entered the picture, but the responsibility remains.

Lewis thought this responsibility important because it gives mankind the "dignity of causality" and lifts us above the level of mere parasites ("Work and Prayer" in GID: 106). God is self-sufficient and doesn't really need us, but he is pleased to give us a small but real part to play. We are "sub-creators," meaning we were made in the image of God the Creator. Now, here on earth, God gives us the opportunity to express that creativity and cause things to happen. He planted a garden once, but only once; since then it's our turn to imitate what he has done and to use what he has made. And in the future, Lewis expected God to continue using us when the time comes for him to redeem all creation from the effects of sin.

I will take up the redemption of creation in chapter seven, but for the present, Lewis urges the ethical treatment of animals. Yes, humanity is above them in the created order, but then angels are above us. "We may find it difficult to formulate a human right of tormenting beasts in terms which would not equally imply an angelic right of tormenting men" ("Vivisection" in GID: 226). Lewis also saw danger not just to animals but to humans as well, since many scientists who cut up animals for research are not Christians, and so for them, humans are just a higher order of animals. "Once the old Christian idea of a total difference in kind between man and beast has been abandoned, then no argument for experiments on animals can be found which is not also an argument for experiments on inferior men" ("Vivisection" in GID: 227). Cruelty to animals may not stop with animals.

Animals in the Space Trilogy

Lewis felt so strongly about the mistreatment of animals and its potential to include humans that he even wrote a plot with himself (as Ransom; both were unmarried, professors, and philologists who enjoyed long walks) as the victim. *Out of the Silent Planet* begins with Ransom out on a walking tour; and, while seeking shelter for the night, he meets up with two unfriendly characters, Devine and Weston, in some sort of altercation with a retarded man named Harry. Angered at Ransom's intrusion, Weston remarks, "We ought to have a dog in this place" (OSP: 12). Devine responds by pointing out that they once did have a dog (named Tartar), but that Weston had already used it in an (evidently fatal!) experiment.

The cause of the struggle with Harry is not at first clear, but we later discover that Devine and Weston have already visited the planet Mars, a world under the authority of a spiritual being called Oyarsa. When Oyarsa summoned Weston and Devine to welcome them to his planet, they were too afraid to go. Since the planet seemed to lack earth's technology, they assumed the inhabitants were savages and suspected they were really looking for a human to sacrifice (OSP: 34, 122). To appease the natives, they returned to earth to get Harry as the sacrifice.

By surprising them in the act, Ransom prevents the abduction of Harry. Devine then recognizes Ransom as a former classmate at Wedenshaw, and they exchange the usual pleasantries. In the course of the conversation, Devine does a little probing and discovers Ransom is alone, on vacation, and wouldn't be missed by anyone for a long time if he didn't return. Always quick to seize an opportunity, Devine puts a drug in Ransom's whiskey. When Ransom later begins to regain consciousness, he overhears Devine urging Weston to abduct Ransom instead of Harry, who is already missed by his mother. At first, Weston is reluctant to do this; after all, Harry is "incapable of serving humanity and only too likely to propagate idiocy," but Ransom is fully "human!" (OSP: 19). But at Devine's urging, Weston overcomes his scruples, Ransom's attempt to escape is prevented, and they set out for Mars with the unwilling Ransom as the new sacrificial victim. What Lewis was warning against in his essay on vivisection has become the plot of the novel. When circumstances allow, scientific research will move from animals to defective people and then even to normal people.

But what lies behind Weston's desire to leave earth and reach other planets? Lewis needs to look no farther than the colonization of various nations by western (perhaps Lewis meant "Weston" to signify "western") cultures over the past few centuries to find the answer. Those who have the power subjugate those who are less advanced to obtain more resources, more *Lebensraum* ("living space"), and even more power. And when there is no more land to claim, then (many believe) humanity must find new worlds before this one dies. Surely not all science is undertaken for this reason, but Lewis does believe that with its powers and promises, science can easily seduce us into thinking that more and more research will eventually conquer ageing and even death. And in our fallen condition, fear of death will lead to – indeed, has already led to – a willingness to sacrifice untold numbers of animals, and, at times, even humans, for the cause.

"Life," explains Weston to the Oyarsa of Mars, "is greater than any system of morality; her claims are absolute. It is not by tribal taboos and copy-book maxims that she has pursued her relentless march from the amoeba to man and from man to civilization" (OSP: 136). Speaking for Lewis, Ransom has a different perspective: "I happen to disagree, even about vivisection" (OSP: 27). Ever the vigilant Christian, Lewis is not convinced by those who believe modern science can ignore human rights in its mission to achieve immortality for the human race. Each individual human has an eternal soul, and so no person has the right to sacrifice another against his will to ensure the survival of humanity.

In *Perelandra*, the next volume of the science fiction trilogy, he presents the positive side of our interaction with animals as well as the negative. Ransom watches the Lady, or Tinidril, the Eve of her planet (Venus), as she lovingly responds to the animals on her world. "There was in her face an authority, in her caress a condescension which by taking seriously the inferiority of her adorers made them somehow less inferior – raised them from the status of pets to that of slaves" (PER: 56).

"The beasts in your world seem almost rational," said Ransom. "We make them older every day," she answered (PER: 56). For Lewis, harmony between man and beast reflects God's will for every world and it is only natural on this unfallen planet. And that includes "raising" the more intelligent animals (making them "older"), not simply coexisting with them. When Lewis describes Ransom back on earth in *That Hideous Strength*, he is careful to point out that Ransom's household has this same harmony with animals – from Mr. Bultitude the bear, to Pinch the cat, and even to mice that appear to remove the crumbs from the floor when summoned by a whistle.

In sharp contrast to the Lady, Weston, who comes to Perelandra possessed by Satan, displays a sickening hatred for every living thing. Ransom first discovers this when he finds the mutilated frog-like creature and, with great difficulty, forces himself to kill it and so end its misery. But the worst is still to come; he discovers a trail of more mutilated frogs and following it finds Weston "quietly and almost surgically inserting his forefinger, with its long sharp nail, under the skin behind the creature's head and ripping it open. Ransom had not noticed before that Weston had such remarkable nails" (PER: 94).

Fingernails like scalpels, creatures like frogs, the animals first used for dissection by nearly every beginning biology student – the connection between vivisection and Weston's gruesome activity on Perelandra is too obvious to overlook.

Further examples of such cruelty in *Perelandra* could be given, but suffice it to say that when Lewis has the opportunity to describe the devil, he goes to great lengths to portray him as having a deep hatred for all life. Surely Lewis is not saying that every scientist involved in vivisection is satanically motivated, but I believe he is implying that an unfeeling cruelty to animals or man, even in the name of science, progress, or whatever, ultimately has its roots in Satan.

In *That Hideous Strength*, Lewis continues to focus on vivisection as he describes the struggle between good and evil. NICE hires Mark to manipulate the public through misleading articles in the press. In this way, carefully avoiding certain words, the real nature of the experiments at Belbury can be concealed. As Feverstone (a new name for Devine, reflecting his ambition to exploit Mars for its gold) puts it:

> ...it does make a difference how things are put. For instance, if it were even whispered that the NICE wanted powers to experiment on criminals, you'd have all the old women of both sexes up in arms and yapping about humanity. Call it re-education of the maladjusted, and you have them all slobbering with delight that the brutal era of retributive punishment has at last come to an end. (THS: 43)

Lewis obviously knew that to oppose vivisection was to appear to many as a "yapping old woman" who derives her only companionship from her dog or cat. Mark sees such people when he and Cosser visit a village destined to be swept away in the name of progress. They see all the riffraff: "The recalcitrant and backward laborer...the wastefully supported pauper...the elderly *rentier* (to make matters worse she had a fat old dog with her)" (THS: 87). Lewis here reminds us that these too are a part of humanity and their lives, humble as they might be, are of eternal value before God. Even for a great scientific cause they must not be sacrificed.

Lewis has made his case by now, but the revenge with which he concludes the Ransom trilogy reveals how deeply he feels about the infliction of pain upon animals. Just as mankind first reached toward the Heavens via the Tower of Babel in hopes of escaping God's judgment should another flood come, so Lewis depicts Belbury, the town where NICE is headquartered, as another concerted effort of man to take his destiny into his own hands, this time through science. To sustain the parallel, Lewis brings upon Belbury the same judgment as Babel received – the confusing of their speech by God. But Lewis adds an extra touch – one which no doubt gave him much satisfaction – a touch not strictly necessary for the plot. He has the magician Merlin, God's instrument, release the animals NICE kept for purposes of experimentation and send them to the banquet hall ready for battle. Their appearance causes panic, and those not killed by the animals are trampled in the stampede.

Merlin has a special mission for Bultitude, Ransom's bear which has been captured by NICE. He is sent to the room where the Head (the "scientific" version of the resurrection) is kept; once there, the bear dispatches Wither and destroys the Head itself. Calamity comes upon NICE from the angelic world as well. The Macrobes, the evil spiritual beings controlling the people of Belbury, have themselves in a sense been practicing vivisection. The human head was removed from its body to become their mouthpiece at their direction. When Belbury falls, the Macrobes continue to manipulate their slaves so as to destroy them now that their usefulness is over. Belbury vivisected animals until they were maimed and broken, and also tried to use fallen angels for their own ends, so poetic justice is served when Lewis brings calamity from above and below.

In reflection, Lewis's emphasis upon vivisection in the Space Trilogy is remarkable. Not only does he persuasively present the arguments for both pro and con positions, but he weaves the theme into the plots of all three novels and even orchestrates revenge without mercy. These subplots testify to the deep love for God's creation that Lewis had, a love which led Lewis to oppose with his head and his heart man's inhumanity to man and to animals – an inhumanity which for Lewis ultimately had its roots in Satan himself.

In the shadow of World War II, the period when Lewis wrote the Space Trilogy, Lewis's passionate feelings on this subject are to be expected. Perhaps more surprising is the lack of response from most Christians to painful experiments on animals which are still widespread today, especially for the testing of cosmetics – hardly a great scientific cause.

But Lewis is deadly serious. The Third Reich convincingly demonstrated how quickly men will turn upon man when the constraints of civilized society are removed. Certainly, Christianity will be threatened with extinction in such circumstances; civilization itself will soon follow.

> If we choose vivisection by rationalizing from within an evolutionary framework, vivisection will win a great advance in the triumph of ruthless, non-moral utilitarianism over the old world of ethical law; a triumph in which we, as well as animals, are already victims, and of which Dachau and Hiroshima mark the more recent achievements. In justifying cruelty to animals we put ourselves on the animal level. We choose the jungle and must abide by that choice. ("Vivisection" in GID: 228)

The Biblical mandate

The message is clear: "Do no unnecessary harm." But what was Lewis suggesting when he had Tinidril say "We make them older every day?" He believed that our God-given responsibility for this planet ("Be fruitful and multiply, and fill the earth and subdue it; and have dominion over ... every living thing that moves upon the earth:" Gen 1:28) means that humans can improve on, or "raise," what God has created. Just as we develop new and better strains of plant life, so also we bring some animals into our houses or pastures, and under our influence they are healthier, they live longer, and develop more personality than ever possible in the wild (PP: 44). Who knows what potential animals might have? "There are (in animals) instincts I had never dreamed of: big with a promise of real morality" ("To Dom Bede Griffiths," L: 422, May 28, 1952).

Only in this context, says Lewis, will the significance of animals fully emerge. "The beasts are to be understood only in their relation to man and, through man, to God" (PP: 138). Why? Because, as noted above, "Man was appointed by God to have dominion over the beasts, and everything a man does to an animal is either a lawful exercise, or a sacrilegious abuse, of an authority by divine right" (PP: 138).

I'm not sure how far Lewis believed the "promise of real morality" could develop in at least some animals, but he does have a point, as any animal lover knows. Once tamed and guided by us, many animals "become" far more than they ever could have in the wild. But how can we help them fulfill their potential for morality or at least some degree of selfhood and personality if we ourselves are immoral in our treatment of them? The answer is Christ's divine life, as Lewis argued in *Mere Christianity*. Once the four cardinal and three Christian virtues have been formed in a person, fair play with others becomes possible. Lewis includes animals in this "others," and by extension, the whole planet itself. Morality must extend to the general purpose of human life, and part of that purpose is our God-given dominion over the natural world.

Nor will that aspect of our purpose die when God makes all things new. Our relationship with creation, including the animals, will increase, in Lewis's view. Somehow, when God raises us in the resurrection, he will also raise the creation, using us to accomplish this and giving us a higher level of the dignity of causality. But this is the subject of chapter seven, so the discussion of the future of animals must end for now.

Has Lewis gone too far in his love of animals? Is there any Biblical basis for how he feels toward them? Well, we certainly won't find in the Scriptures any passage that comes close to a modern understanding of ecology, but there are clues nevertheless. Lewis does accurately reflect Genesis 1:26–30, the passage where God gives mankind dominion over fish, birds, and land animals. And in Genesis 2, God acknowledges that Adam is alone and that he needs a suitable partner. But before God creates Eve, he brings birds and land animals before Adam so that he can give them names. Names are very important in a Biblical context, and the understanding here would be that Adam was able to give a name appropriate for the kind of animal before him and also had the authority to do so. Lewis includes this same authority in Perelandra, his imaginary version of the Garden of Eden. Ransom hears Tor, the Adam of the planet, mention a place by name. "And Ransom realized that the King had uttered not an observation but an enactment" (PER: 180).

The name-giving in Genesis also served to reveal to Adam, and all of his descendants, that animals are close enough to us for us to relate to them, even give names to them, and yet none of them have the potential to be the compatible helper we need, including a sexual partner. So God creates Eve, and when Adam sees her, we get another glimpse into his perceptiveness. He recognizes that she is made from the same flesh and bones as he, and so is on the same level as he (Gen 2:23). As such, she will be the helper that he needs and will rule over the animals with him.

The next significant interaction between God and man comes when Moses receives the law to give to the tribes of Israel. A significant part of the Torah has to do with the land. God makes it clear to begin with that the land belongs to him

(Lev 25:23). He also explains to Israel that he is displacing the cultures that live in Canaan and giving the land to them instead because of their immoral lifestyle, which included taking animals as sexual partners. Their practices are so evil that the land itself is attempting to expel them, and if the Israelites adopt the same practices, the land will also turn on them (Lev 18:24–30). But if they observe God's laws, God will bless the land so that it will yield plentiful crops.

Perhaps it seems rather strange for God to be concerned about dirt. But he is for our sakes: our natural lives depend upon the soil, and God intends to achieve his purposes with us here in this natural environment. If we are to prosper, we must till the land with care and wisely manage the animals we use for food, clothes, assistance in our labor, and companionship. Out of concern for us, God established the week of six days of work and one day of rest. And he also told Israel to let the land rest for a year after cultivating it for six years; thus giving the land the same amount of rest as humans. And we see the beginnings of wildlife management in the law; when the Israelites came upon a nest, they could take the young but were not to harm the mother. Why? So that "it will go well with you and you may live long" (Deut 22:6–7).

- To be human, then, is to share a physical nature with the beasts.
- To be fully human is to rule over this planet and care for it, including the animals.
- To be fallen makes this responsibility more difficult, but the responsibility remains.

Lewis faithfully reflects this Biblical perspective. He reminds us that our relationship with God includes our relationship with what he has made, and this relationship, including animals and ecology, should be a part of Christian theology.

Humans and Angels

Fallen angels

> I sometimes wonder if we have even begun to understand what
> is involved in the very concept of creation. If God will create, He
> will make something to be, and yet to be not Himself. To be
> created is, in some sense, to be ejected or separated. Can it be that
> the more perfect the creature is, the further this separation must
> at some point be pushed? It is saints, not common people, who
> experience the "dark night." It is men and angels, not beasts,
> who rebel. Inanimate matter sleeps in the bosom of the Father.
>
> (LTM: 44)

Lewis approached angels as he did many other topics, with a
combination of logic and Biblical truth augmented by imagination. He believed in their existence, and he accepted the New
Testament perspective, more fully developed than in the Old,
of one fallen angel, with the title of Satan (accuser or slan-
derer), leading other fallen angels in a rebellion against God.
Lewis follows Scripture in referring to these angels as devils,
but it's difficult to tell from his writings if he distinguished
between devils and demons. He certainly would have noticed
the many references to them in the gospels, but for his purposes, the important thing was to contrast between good and
evil rather than get into details that would complicate the
discussion.

Biblical references to fallen angels, including Satan, made
sense to Lewis. They, not God, were responsible for much of
the evil that persuaded the pre-Christian Lewis to be an atheist. But Satan is not God's equal, as we found in chapter three.
Any being that chooses to do evil must have such things as
existence, intelligence, and will, and is using those good qualities for bad purposes. Badness, then, is only spoiled goodness

that originally came from God, and this is why Satan is not
God's equal (MC: 34–5).

Yet Satan fascinated Lewis, as his poetry shows. An angel
that challenges God must be powerful indeed; an angel
that has so deeply affected our world must be intelligent
and following a plan. Compared to him, we are weak and
half-hearted sinners, often partly ignorant of what we are
doing, and thoughtlessly sinning because we blindly follow
the examples of others, not because we really want to.

> Thou only art alternative to God, oh dark
> And burning island among spirits...
> Only thy absolute lust is worth the thinking of.
> All else is weak disguising of the wishful heart...
> Lord, open not too often my weak eyes to this.
> ("Wormwood" in P: 87)

The Christian understanding of Satan is that he, joined by
other fallen angels, now works to frustrate the purposes of
God. If he is not strong enough to directly attack an omnipotent God, he can express his rebellion by focusing upon God's
creation – especially us, the object of his love. But how can
fallen creatures manage to work together, Lewis asks, and
what can they do to us humans? Lewis gives his views on
these subjects in *The Screwtape Letters*, an imaginary correspondence between devils which has become a classic.

In *The Screwtape Letters*, all of the thirty-one letters are written by Screwtape (a senior devil with many successes to his
credit) to Wormwood, a junior devil who has been given his
first human "patient." Screwtape gives Wormwood much
practical advice, but things go from bad to worse. The patient
becomes a Christian and falls in love with a Christian woman.
Before Wormwood can reclaim him from the Enemy (God),
his patient is killed by a bomb during World War II.

Wormwood comes for the patient's soul after his death, but it is too late and he will pay for his failure by becoming food for other devils.

Scripture does not directly explain how Satan coordinates his efforts with other devils, but Lewis finds a plausible explanation by observing fallen humanity.

> Bad angels, like bad men, are entirely practical. They have two motives. The first is fear of punishment . . . Their second motive is a kind of hunger. I feign that devils can, in a spiritual sense, eat one another; and us. Even in human life we have seen the passion to dominate, almost to digest, one's fellow . . . In Hell . . . the stronger spirit – there are perhaps no bodies to impede the operation – can really and irrevocably suck the weaker into itself and permanently gorge its own being on the weaker's outraged personality. (SL: xi)

The principle Lewis found in human and diabolical societies is the domination of the weaker by the stronger. And this absorption of the will resembles the physical act of ingesting food. So, Lewis stresses, when a human relationship has deteriorated into the domination of one by the other, and the acceptance of such domination – and such co-dependent relationships are common – a little bit of Hell is coming into being on earth.

Lewis returned to *The Screwtape Letters* seventeen years later when he added Screwtape's commencement address at the Tempter's Training College. Through Screwtape's remarks Lewis is commenting on the sad condition of the world. Education has become so deficient and the church so weak that most people today are, in Screwtape's view, only "vermin . . . muddled in mind," "undersexed morons," and "residual puddles of what once was soul" (SPT: 155–6). Conditioned by advertising to conform and following rock stars and other charismatic celebrities, they thoughtlessly fall into adultery with others, accept bribes at work, and so forth with scarcely a thought about right and wrong. From Screwtape's perspective, feeding on such souls makes for a very insipid meal, but at least the banquet makes up in quantity for what it lacks in quality.

After the meal comes the toast, and Screwtape is glad to find there are still some bottles of "vintage Pharisee" to enjoy. The wine owes its quality to Satan's success in undermining Christianity itself; a major triumph indeed! Those who reduced the faith to "rules, relics and rosaries" are now against their will blended together with others who reduced the gospel to legalities like abstinence from wine, cards and the theatre. "How they hated each other up there where the sun shone! How much more they hate each other now that they are forever conjoined but not reconciled" (SPT: 171).

The point of this infernal correspondence is that we are loved by God and are therefore targets of God's enemies. The message is not one of hopeless despair, even though fallen angels are much more powerful than we. God's protection is always present; otherwise, fallen angels could easily overcome humanity. Fortunately, they have very limited access to us, as Lewis indicates in several letters when Wormwood's patient receives divine aid at crucial times. Nor does Lewis think that humans would be less vulnerable to the enemy if only we did not have bodies. Satan will attack by that route if he can; think of gluttony and sexual immorality, for example. But the excellent wine for Screwtape's toast did not come from those kinds of sins, but from the hatred of Catholics for Protestants and vice versa.

Lewis gladly owns up to being an amphibian because God made him that way. What God creates is good, and since Satan can't himself create anything, he can only tempt us to use what we are, body or soul, in ways, times, or degrees that God has forbidden. What is "straight" must be twisted. And the animal parts of us have their physical limitations. We can only eat so much. But what we share with the angels, Lewis cautions us, has more potential for evil. What limit does the body impose upon envy, greed, selfish ambition, sloth, spite, and, of course, pride – the sin Satan knows best? None whatsoever.

How can humans avoid being a "meal" for the enemy? Lewis has already given the answer: by letting God replace the sinful nature with his divine nature. "I have come that you might have life, and have it abundantly" (John 10:10). And that nature is "full and flows over." In contrast, devils are "empty and would be filled" (SL: 38). Lewis had John's words in mind when he had Satan say through Weston in *Perelandra*, "it is for this that I came here, that you may have Death in abundance" (PER: 98; the opposite of John 10:10). Life or death, fullness or emptiness, domination of others or serving them; these are the choices Lewis emphasizes throughout his writings.

Good angels

Given the infernal perspective of *The Screwtape Letters*, it's not surprising that good angels are mostly ignored in that correspondence. But Lewis often wrote about them elsewhere, and accepted their presence in the universe. Like humans, they have God-given responsibilities, including guiding heavenly bodies to ensure their regular movement. This in turn preserves the regularity of seasons and years for us. Pre-Christian Jews believed the same.

Like us, angels have minds, but unlike us, no bodies. They are therefore spirits, or "naked minds." "We have an immediate and intuitive grasp only of axioms and have to seek all other knowledge by the laborious process of discursive thinking. They are wholly intuitive; concepts are as palpable to them as apples or pennies are to us. In fact, their reason is to ours as noon to dusk" ("Imagination and Thought" in SMRL: 53).

In medieval Christian theology, angels are arranged into a hierarchy, and most of these "ranks" have nothing to do with us. Lewis lists the highest three as Seraphim, Cherubim, and Thrones, and these spirit beings guard the throne of God and offer unceasing praise. The next group consists of Domin-ations, Virtues, and Powers. These oversee nature; we might call them the deacons of the universe. The lowest classes are involved with human affairs. Principalities guide the destiny of nations, and Archangels and Angels are concerned with indi-viduals. Lewis notes that the angel Gabriel who was sent to Mary to tell her she would bear a son is identified as an Archangel (Luke 1:26–38; "Imagination and Thought" in SMRL: 53–4). Lewis knew, of course, that the Bible was not so specific as to give us such a hierarchy, but it does mention many ranks or kinds of spirit beings and it logically follows that they relate to each other in some kind of hierarchical order.

Lewis speaks of the part good angels play in the human drama when Wormwood's patient in *The Screwtape Letters* dies. He begins to look around in the spirit world and sees good angels for the first time.

> He had no faintest conception till that very hour of how they would look, and even doubted their existence. But when he saw them he knew that he had always known them and real-ized what part each one of them had played at many an hour in his life when he had supposed himself alone, so that now he could say to them, one by one, not "Who *are* you" but "So it was *you* all the time." (SL: 147)

Angels are prominent all through Biblical history, and Lewis assumes they still play a (generally invisible) part both in the course of nations and individual human lives. As Hebrews 1:14 asks of angels: "Are they not all ministering spirits sent to serve in behalf of those who are about to inherit salvation?" Thankfully, we are not alone in what Lewis called the Great War.

Between Animals and Angels

In conclusion, Lewis preferred to view humanity not in isolation, but in terms of what mankind shares with the animal kingdom and with angels. This unique place in the order of creation makes possible fellowship with and responsibility for the beasts, and also the potential for life in the spirit world and fellowship with God. The body is not a source of sin or something Christians should be ashamed of; Lewis forcefully rejects Gnosticism. Bodies do after all have some privileges not even angels enjoy.

> ...the senses' witchery
> Guards us, like air, from Heavens too big to see...
> Yet here, within this tiny, charm'd interior,
> This parlour of the brain, their Maker shares
> With living men some secrets in a privacy
> Forever ours, not theirs.
>   ("On Being Human" in P: 35)

Only through the body come the beauties of nature and only by means of it can humanity fulfill its God-given responsibility to care for this world. And both body and soul have a future in the theology of Lewis. Until then, both must be guarded against the techniques of Screwtape. Edmund's desire to rule over his brother and sisters (pride of soul) played on the appetites of his body and made him susceptible to the lure of Turkish Delight. The addiction brought him under the power of the White Witch, and he betrayed his own sisters and brother.

Chapter 5

Walking by Faith

"The professor believed Lucy was telling the truth."
Illustration © 2007 by Deborah Wilson Camp

Poor Lucy! No one believed her when she told her brothers and sister about the new world she discovered at the back of the wardrobe in the spare room. Even after Edmund visited Narnia, things didn't get any better. Out of pure meanness, he told the others that he and Lucy were only pretending. Lucy ran from the room in tears. In the morning, Peter and Susan decide to visit the professor, who listens carefully to the whole story.

As they discuss the possibility that Lucy is lying, they admit to the professor that Lucy always has been the one who told the truth, not Edmund. So then might she be mad? After all, a strange world at the back of a wardrobe is rather unusual, to say the least. But the professor observes: "One has only to look at her and talk to her to see that she is not mad" (LWW: 45). The children don't know what to say; the only other choice is so unbelievable.

> Logic! Said the Professor half to himself. Why don't they teach logic at these schools? There are only three possibilities. Either your sister is telling lies, or she is mad, or she is telling the truth. You know she doesn't tell lies and it is obvious that she is not mad. For the moment then and unless any further evidence turns up, we must assume that she is telling the truth. (LWW: 45)

But, the children protest, she was gone for only a minute or so; there wasn't time for her to have hours of adventures.

> That is the very thing that makes her story so likely to be true, said the Professor. If there really is a door in this house that leads to some other world...I should not be at all surprised to find that that other world had a separate time of its own; so that however long you stayed there it would never take up any of *our* time. On the other hand, I don't think many girls of her age would invent that idea of themselves. If she had been pretending, she would have hidden for a reasonable time before coming out and telling her story. (LWW: 46)

All this is quite remarkable. Lewis, a highly educated university professor, is teaching that the intellect, informed by the senses, is not always an accurate guide when God is involved. His ways, and nature, are above our understanding. In fact, the mind can even get in the way of our faith. Lewis thought this so important he wrote at least a dozen definitions of faith. Essentially, they all come down to this: believing God and his word despite moods that change, the intellect that questions, difficult circumstances – anything that would challenge the truthfulness of God.

The Myth of Cupid and Psyche According to Apuleius

Lewis was attracted to myths both before and after his conversion because they often contained "divine truth falling on human imagination" (M: 139). He was particularly fascinated by the myth *Metamorphoses* or *The Golden Ass*, written by Lucius Apuleius Platonicus in the second century of the Christian era, but perhaps originating much earlier. This particular story did not involve the death and reviving of a god that benefited the world, but Lewis did find in it insights that would benefit Christians. He adapted the story to emphasize what he viewed as important, and expanded it into a novel told from the perspective of a woman.

Apuleius wrote about the marriage of Cupid and Psyche. Cupid was the son of Venus, the goddess of love, and Psyche was the youngest of three daughters born to a king and queen. She was so beautiful that people neglected the worship of Venus. In her jealousy, Venus ordered her son Cupid, who already had a reputation for mischief for shooting people who were incompatible with his arrows, to do likewise to Psyche, so that she would fall in love with the worst sort of man.

The plan went awry when Cupid looked upon her beauty. Falling in love with her, he prepared a palace for her with every luxury provided. The love was mutual, but he visited her only during the night, for she was not to see his face. In time, Psyche asked that her sisters be allowed to visit, and Cupid gave reluctant consent. They enjoyed the richness of the palace but were consumed by jealousy and plotted to ruin her happiness. Her husband must be a terrible serpent; why else does he conceal his appearance?

Cupid finally gave in to their logic, and uncovered a lamp to gaze upon his face. But a drop of oil fell from the lamp upon his shoulder, he awoke, rebuked her, and vanished. In her despair, Psyche tried to drown herself, but the god Pan prevented her, telling her not to try again. Eventually, she fell into Venus's power, who treated her like a slave and gave her impossible tasks to complete. First, she had to sort out large stacks of seeds and was aided by ants. Next, she was sent to get golden wool from dangerous sheep. A reed by a river bank showed her where some of their wool had been caught on the bushes.

The third task was to bring a cup of water from the river Styx in the underworld, and this task was accomplished for her by an eagle. Finally, Venus sent her to the underworld to bring back in a box the beauty of Persephone, the Queen of the Dead. Guided by a voice, and told never to look within the box, she was able to find it. But curiosity overcame her on the way back, she looked within, and became unconscious. But the story had a happy ending; Cupid forgave her, Jupiter agreed to allow the marriage, and Psyche became a goddess. Even Venus was reconciled to her; probably because Psyche, no longer among the mortals, ceased to be her competition.

The Myth According to Lewis

Lewis regarded Apuleius as the transmitter of the story, not its creator, and so he felt "quite free to go behind Apuleius"

(TWHF: 313) and change some of the plot to add details or bring out more clearly aspects of the myth that could support a Christian perspective. The expanded myth became the novel *Till We Have Faces*, and Lewis tells the story from the perspective of Orual, the very homely, oldest daughter of a king who is both cruel and cowardly. Orual has two sisters, Redival and Psyche, the youngest.

The story unfolds in a pagan kingdom where the native religion is the worship of Ungit, represented by a "black stone without head or hands or a face," and believed to be "a very strong goddess" (TWHF: 4). Ungit often requires blood sacrifices and to Orual, her religion seems dark, mysterious, and demanding. Even though the king often consults the priest who represents Ungit, tragedies still come to the palace. After his first wife died, his second wife also died within a year of their marriage, after giving birth to Psyche. The king is furious with the priest, but fears the revenge of Ungit, and so he vents his fury upon his family.

Later, when things have calmed down, the king sends to Greece, a near-by kingdom, and hires a tutor for his three daughters. (Perhaps Lewis was thinking of Philip, king of Macedonia, who hired Aristotle from neighboring Greece to teach his son Alexander the Great.) They call him the Fox, and come to love and respect him. But when prolonged drought plagues the kingdom, Orual's father consults the priest of Ungit who tells him that rain will return if one of his daughters is sacrificed to the monster who lives up in the mountains. The cowardly king, relieved that his life was not required, agrees to sacrifice Psyche, the purest and most beautiful of his three daughters, to save the kingdom.

The horrible deed is carried out and Psyche disappears, eaten by the monster, or so it is believed. But in reality, invisible beings bring her to a marvelous palace, where she becomes the bride of Cupid. Her every wish is granted, and she lacks for nothing in that beautiful place. But there is one condition to the marriage: she must not see the face of the god. Meanwhile, Orual decides to slip away to the place where Psyche had been sacrificed to discover if there are any remains of her. Accompanied by Bardia, one of the palace soldiers, they reach the dreaded place, only to find no trace of Psyche whatsoever. Thinking she might have been dragged away, they widen the search until they finally come to a river. There, on the other side, tanned and healthy, stands Psyche.

Soon Orual learns that Psyche did not die, but rather Zephyrus, the god of the West-wind, freed her from her chains and carried her away to a palace. After hearing her story, Orual, wanting to believe but not yet able, asks if she can see the palace. Psyche is stunned, for they are standing on the stairs of the great gate of the palace. How can she not see the palace? Orual wonders if Psyche is mad, and yet even her eyes tell her Psyche has encountered the divine. "From the top of her head to her naked feet she was bathed in life and beauty and well-being. It was as if they flowed over her or from her" (TWHF: 123).

Later that night, unable to sleep, Orual returns to the river's edge, and for a brief moment, sees the palace. "As she [Psyche] had said, it was like no house ever seen in our land or age. Pinnacles and buttresses leaped up – no memories of mine, you would think, could help me to imagine them – unbelievably tall and slender, pointed and prickly as if stone were shooting out into branch and flower" (TWHF: 132).

What a predicament Orual finds herself in; what should she believe? Her beloved sister has not been eaten by a monster and seems more alive than ever. But is she sane, claiming to be the wife of a god? To make matters worse, she herself has seen the palace, if only for a moment, but can she trust her eyes? Orual does what most of us would do; she asks the significant people around her. First, she consults Bardia, who has been her protector on the journey. His cautious answer represents many whose idea of religion is to not give God any problems. "It's not my way to say more than I can help of gods and divine matters... I think the less Bardia meddles with the gods, the less they'll meddle with Bardia" (TWHF: 135). Pushing him for more help, Orual asks what he thinks about a god who forbids his bride to see his face. Reflecting for a time, Bardia finally concludes that the reason is that Psyche would be repelled by what she saw. In sum, Bardia appears to be a "solid," dependable person on the surface, but his "religion" is based upon fear and distrust. The less contact with the gods, the better.

The two travelers return to the palace, and soon the Fox, the tutor of the three sisters, comes to learn of any news they might have. Orual recounts her experiences, but does not tell him that she saw Psyche's palace. The Fox rejoices at hearing Psyche is still alive, but soon his face becomes sad and concerned when Orual tells him that Psyche believes she is married to a god and living in a splendid palace. The tutor is no Platonist, for he believes that only what the senses can perceive is real. If Psyche is healthy, someone must be feeding her. Since that someone could not be an invisible god, then it must be some mountain man who comes to her in the dark. And since Psyche believes him, the experience of being exposed on the mountain as prey for some monster must have driven her mad. It's all very neatly reasoned out, but far from the truth! Reason will never have eyes to see Psyche's palace.

Now Orual has heard from the two wisest persons she knows, and both explanations seem true to her. But they do agree on one thing: something terrible has happened to Psyche, and Orual resolves to act. She must rescue Psyche from this person or monster who refuses to show his face, and if Psyche is out of her mind, Orual is willing to use force. But before she can return to Psyche, she remembers what she saw and a part of her mind says to her:

> Do not meddle. Anything might be true. You are among marvels that you do not understand. Carefully, carefully. Who knows what ruin you might pull down on her head and yours? But with the other part of me I answered that I was indeed her mother and her father, too (all she had of either), that my love must be grave and provident, not slip-shod and indulgent, that there is a time for love to be stern. (TWHF: 152)

Orual's refusal to believe in the spirit world or in the goodness of the gods, combined with her possessive and controlling "love" of others, leads her to the conviction that "tough love" is what the situation calls for. When she meets Psyche once again, she tries to convince her that her husband is either a monster or perhaps a criminal; after all, both Bardia and the Fox agree. Now the contrast of faith and sight becomes clear as they converse. For Orual, anyone who forbids his wife to see his face has something sinister to hide. For Psyche, the ways of the gods are above us and we must trust that they have good reasons for their prohibitions. Without realizing, Orual has taken the position of the serpent in the Garden of Eden, who told Eve that God didn't want her to eat of a certain tree because he didn't want anyone else to be as wise as him. In other words, God can't be trusted, and disobedience will prove it.

And so Orual tells Psyche the only way to prove she is married to a god is to look upon his face. When Psyche refuses, Orual takes out her dagger and pushes the point completely through her arm to demonstrate her resolve. If Psyche refuses, she will kill her and then end her own life as well. Out of love for Orual, Psyche agrees to look upon the face of Cupid. Soon there is a tremendous cry, thunder and lightning, the palace collapses, the god appears and rebukes Orual, and the sobs of

Psyche are heard in the distance. Now she must wander over the face of the earth as an outcast, and spend her life attempting to complete the tasks Venus imposes upon her.

Orual returns home, still unwilling to accept the glimpse of the palace across the river and what she has heard from Cupid himself. Psyche is dead to her now. She enters Psyche's room and puts everything as it had been before tragedy struck. She finds what appears to be a hymn to the god of the mountain and destroys it. That part of Psyche she will not accept. Her jewels and clothes from childhood Orual does keep, neatly arranged in their proper places. Then she shuts the door to Psyche's room, and locks and seals it.

Orual also rearranges her inner life. She turns to the study of natural sciences because "I wanted hard things now, and to pile up knowledge . . . My aim was to build up more and more that strength, hard and joyless, which had come to me when I heard the god's sentence . . . to drive all the woman out of me" (TWHF: 184). She succeeds in this, and after her father's death, becomes queen and rules the kingdom well.

The third change Orual makes, and perhaps the most significant symbol of her post-Psyche life, is her veil. She first wore it during her two trips to the mountain so she could remain secret, but then decided to make it a permanent part of her attire. In time, people forgot her ugly appearance and imagination took over. Some thought the veil must cover a face too hideous to behold, others, no face at all. Still others supposed men would go mad if they saw her beauty, but in the end, she was a mysterious and fearful person to all, which added to her authority.

Many years pass and as Orual nears the end of her life, and with her kingdom of Glome in peace, she decides to visit other lands. During her journey she comes to a small temple and within she finds a statue of a woman with a black veil over her face. (Her own veil is white.) She asks the priest of the temple about this strange goddess, and he begins to tell the story of how a mortal woman recently became divine. Orual is shocked by what she hears, for it is her own story.

But the priest tells her story badly, saying that the sisters of Psyche were able to see Cupid's palace. Orual is outraged: a story like that belongs to another world, where the gods do show themselves to mortals and do not ask men to believe what contradicts what our senses report. In such a world Orual would have been faultless! Challenging the priest's version of the myth, she asks why the sisters would have ruined Psyche's happiness if they were able to see where she lived. Because they were jealous, the priest replies. Orual refuses to see jealousy in herself and leaves the temple in anger. But she is unable to forget the story and now has even more accusations to bring before the gods.

Not long after returning home, old and tired, her father suddenly appears to her, bossy as ever, and commands her to get up. They go to the Pillar Room and he commands her to dig. They both dig and presently break through the floor, only to find another room beneath it. They jump down into the room, smaller and warmer than the room above, and once again she is told to dig. Now the dirt is hard clay, but they finally manage to dig through the floor, only to find yet another, still smaller room. Once down there, the room starts to shrink and Orual fears being suffocated, but the king ignores the danger and brings her to a mirror on the wall. "Who is Ungit?" he asks. No longer veiled, Orual looks . . . and sees not her face but that of Ungit. "Without question it was true. It was I who was Ungit. That ruinous face was mine. I was . . . that all-devouring womblike, yet barren, thing. Glome was a web – I the swollen spider, squat at its center, gorged with men's stolen lives" (TWHF: 276).

Pondering what this might mean, Orual resolves that she will not be Ungit. She will practice true philosophy, as Socrates

taught, and so transform her soul into a thing of beauty
(TWHF: 282). But every effort is unsuccessful; why won't
the gods help her? Soon in her dreams she finds herself trying
to accomplish some of the tasks given to Psyche, only to fail.
Lying in a desert, unable to rise, a divine eagle approaches and
asks about the roll in her hands. It is her book, and she tells the
bird that it contains her complaints against the gods. Instantly,
she is brought before them, and finally has the chance to be
heard. Out pours all the pent-up hatred and spite:

> You know well that I never really began to hate you until
> Psyche began talking of her palace and her lover and her
> husband . . . the girl was mine. What right had you to steal
> her away into your dreadful heights . . . there's no room for
> you and us in the same world. You're a tree in whose shadow
> we can't thrive. We want to be our own. I was my own
> and Psyche was mine and no one else had any right to
> her . . . "Enough," said the judge . . . "Are you answered?" he
> said. "Yes," said I. (TWHF: 290–3)

More self-discovery comes when Orual in a vision sees the
Fox. He guides her to a place filled with beautiful pictures, and
as they gaze at the picture of woman coming to a river bank, it
comes to life. Soon Orual recognizes the woman; she is Psyche
and each picture shows them her life after she left Cupid's
palace. After Psyche completes each task, finally returning
from the underworld with the beauty of Persephone in a
box, they discuss her life of suffering.

> "Did we really do these things to her?" I asked.
> "Yes. All here's true."
> "And we said we loved her."
> "And we did. She had no more dangerous enemies than us.
> And in that far distant day when the gods become wholly
> beautiful, or we at last are shown how beautiful they always

were, this will happen more and more. For mortals, as you said, will become more and more jealous. And mother and wife and child and friend will all be in league to keep a soul from being united with the Divine Nature." (TWHF: 304)

The Fox then leads Orual outside, where she finally meets Psyche. Falling at her feet, Orual says: "Never again will I call you mine; but all there is of me shall be yours" (TWHF: 305). As they are reconciled to each other, Orual senses the approach of the divine. The old Orual is unmade, and then transformed by the arrows of the god. Looking down into the pool at their feet she sees two people, both beautiful, reflected in the water. A great voice proclaims: "You also are Psyche" (TWHF: 308). Orual's death follows four days later.

The Meaning of the Myth

Why did Lewis choose this myth? As a Christian and even before his conversion he was attracted to the stories of gods who died, came to life again, and somehow helped the world. The myth of Cupid and Psyche does not tell such a story, yet it held his fascination for decades and is the only myth he made into a novel, and did so, the biographers tell us, with much assistance from his wife, Joy.

Natural affection

One reason Lewis liked this story is that he found it to be an ideal vehicle for what he wanted to say about human affection. The two sisters were so jealous of Psyche that they were willing to spoil her happiness. As Lewis shapes the story, only one sister embodies this spite, since the story is told through the voice of Orual, but the message is the same. Orual serves as an example of natural affection, one of the loves Lewis described so well in *The Four Loves*. When Orual and Psyche were together, their affection for each other was tender and strong. But when the gods took Psyche, that same affection, because it was only natural and therefore lacked divine support, became possessive.

> What such love particularly cannot stand is to see the beloved passing into a sphere where it cannot follow... Someone becomes a Christian, or, in a family nominally Christian already, does something like becoming a missionary or entering a religious order. The others suffer a sense of outrage. What they love is being taken from them! The boy must be mad! And the conceit of him! Or is there something in it after all? Let's hope it is only a phase! ("Letter to Clyde S. Kilby" in L: 462–3, February 10, 1957)

Lewis returned to this theme (which shows its importance to him) in the "Affection" chapter of *The Four Loves*. Affection dislikes change. "Few things in the ordinary peacetime life of a civilized country are more nearly fiendish than the rancour with which a whole unbelieving family will turn on the one member of it who has become a Christian... "He who was one of Us has become one of Them. What right had anybody to do it? He is *ours*" (FL: 46–7).

Lewis's insights into the reaction of natural affection when the family circle (one type of "inner ring") is broken also explain why Jesus said his own message would be so divisive: "Do not think that I have come to bring peace to the earth; I have not come to bring peace, but a sword. For I have come to set a man against his father, and a daughter against her mother, and a daughter-in-law against her mother-in-law; and one's foes will be members of one's own household" (Matthew 10:34–36).

The importance of faith

But why do families react so strongly when one of them changes? Yes, affection dislikes change and there may be jealously involved. But underneath it all is the fact of a new reality that the others are not able to see. At the end of *Till We Have Faces* Lewis tells us that even when he read the story for the first time, he realized something was wrong. The older sisters should not have been able to see the palace Cupid made for Psyche. So Lewis made it invisible (though he gave Orual a glimpse of it) and regarded this change as the "central alteration in my own version" (TWHF: 313).

With this change, the story becomes more consistent with the other parts of the story that serve the Christian message so well. Towering over everything is the theme that surely caught and held the attention of even the pre-Christian Lewis: the destiny of Psyche (the Greek word for soul) is to be married to a god. And once Lewis became a believer, how could he not return to the story and make the necessary corrections so that it could more accurately reflect its divine source?

But such a marriage, described as the marriage supper of the Lamb in the Bible, is possible only on one condition: Psyche, that is, the soul, must not see the face of God. Faith, not logic based on the evidence our senses report to us, makes this union possible, for "without faith it is impossible to please God" (Heb 11:6). Lewis brought the Fox into the story to represent the logic made so famous by Greek philosophy, and sure enough, when Orual consults him after seeing Psyche, he turns her away from what the soul understood. And so she turns to "masculine" pursuits that will give her the empirical evidence the mind demands.

Orual not only turned away from faith, her possessive affection brought about the "fall" of Psyche when she forced her to view the face of Cupid. As Eve was driven from the Garden of Eden, Psyche may no longer enjoy the luxuries of the palace and the presence of her lover. Now the gods set seemingly impossible tasks for her as she wanders the earth, and our first parents likewise find that their disobedience results in a much harder existence.

Yet even after disaster, the gods help Psyche, and we have not been abandoned either. The promise of reunion remains; Cupid is still smitten by the beauty of the soul. And Jesus still intends to return for his bride, the church, even though she has "no beauty but what the Bride-groom gives her; he does not find, but makes her, lovely" (FL: 105).

But first, the veil must come off. Orual kept insisting that God show himself, but only when she unveiled herself to God did she find the answers she was seeking, and discover that she, not God, had been the problem all along. In *The Great Divorce*, Spirits came down from the mountains of Heaven to help the Ghosts become more solid. Lewis uses the same technique in *Faces* when he brings help to Orual in the person of her deceased father. He makes her finally remove the veil, and they begin to dig down into her self, past the superego, down into the ego, and deeper still until they finally reach the id, that ugly troll that lives under the bridge between the heart and the mind. The sight of her possessive self is a crucial step in her becoming what God wants her to be: another Psyche, and beautiful at last.

Reconciling faith and sight

Lewis hasn't given up on the mind. It too comes from God. But the mind weighs what the senses report to it, and God is (usually) not perceived by the senses. When the soul reports what the senses cannot, the mind must be humble enough to admit that the divine is beyond its scope. And when the mind accepts what it cannot verify by reason, that person has taken a "step of faith." Then something interesting happens. After conversion, new insights begin to flood into the mind and Christianity starts making sense. Now the mind does have a legitimate role to play. For Lewis, the faith was like the sun rising; not that he was looking at the sun, but that by it he could see, that is, begin to really understand for the first time the world around him.

In the story, Orual was caught between the "dark" or "thick" religion of Ungit who demanded mysterious blood sacrifices, and the "clear" or "thin" philosophy of the Fox who reduced the divine to logic. "I was the child of Glome and the pupil of the Fox; I saw that for years my life had been lived in two halves, never fitted together" (TWHF: 151). By choosing the latter and denying what her soul reported about the palace of Cupid, she separated herself from the divine. Lewis divided religions into either of these two categories, and believed that a true religion must contain both. Since Cupid's castle was a divine construction, Lewis needed to change the myth and make it invisible to the senses. In this way he made the story more Christian, the only religion that successfully combines both thick and thin in the lives of believers.

> The true God must have made both the child and the man, both the savage and the citizen, both the head and the belly. Christianity . . . takes a convert from central Africa and tells him to obey an enlightened universalistic ethic: it takes a twentieth-century academic prig like me and tells me to go fasting to a Mystery, to drink the blood of the Lord. The savage convert has to be Clear: I have to be Thick. That is how one knows one has come to the real religion. ("Christian Apologetics" in GID: 102–3)

It must not have been easy for Lewis – who possessed such a powerful intellect – to admit that faith is a better way than sight to approach the divine. The danger he warned against is assuming the mind that helped Orual become a capable ruler should also guide her in understanding God and what he is doing. When change came to Orual's life, her jealousy overcame any trust in the divine. Moreover, she thought only of herself instead of the happiness of Psyche, who was glad to go to the Mountain, the place of beauty she had longed for all her life (Lewis used the German word *Sehnsucht* to refer to this deep-seated, inner longing for joy that he first experienced as a child). The gods were there, she was going to her lover (TWHF: 75). This, then, is the message from the Divine to pre-Christian pagans that Lewis saw in the myth of Cupid and Psyche. God isn't a fearful ogre ready to send plagues upon us if we don't sacrifice our children to him. He plans to make us beautiful, body and soul, and unite us to himself.

Chapter 6

God's Plan for the Soul

"The food is terrible!"
Illustration © 2007 by Deborah Wilson Camp

"Aslan," said Lucy through her tears, "could you – will you – do something for these Dwarfs?" "Dearest," said Aslan, "I will show you both what I can and what I cannot do." Then Aslan growled, but the Dwarfs heard only a strange sound at the other end of the Stable. Then Aslan shook his mane and a glorious feast appeared. The Dwarfs began eating, but it seemed to them that they were eating only hay, raw cabbage, turnips, and drinking dirty water.

"You see," said Aslan. "They will not let us help them. They have chosen cunning instead of belief. Their prison is in their own minds, yet they are in that prison, and so afraid of being taken in that they cannot be taken out."

(LB: 146–8)

Well, I can sympathize with the Dwarfs because I don't like to be deceived either, and they were certainly led astray by Tash, a type of Satan in *The Last Battle*. But did that unfortunate experience have to end so badly? Of course not. None of us is perfect, and so we all make errors in thought (and deed!) – even the brightest of us. Sometimes what we say can influence others to believe something we thought was true, but wasn't. But we mustn't let such experiences make us cynical because the only way to learn and grow is to think about new ideas, and that means taking a risk. We might be fooled again. But the important thing is to *want* to know the truth. Sooner or later, Lewis (and the Bible) tells us, those who seek will surely find. The Dwarves stopped believing in anything but themselves. Finally, not even Aslan could reach them.

But is playing safe a sin? Is cynicism wrong if it guards a person from being deceived? Lewis answers this question in *The Great Divorce* when he meets (in his dream) a tall, lean, hardbitten Ghost on the outskirts of Heaven. He strikes Lewis as the reliable sort, and so they begin conversing. The Ghost tells Lewis he has been just about everywhere, and all of the scenic places on earth are just advertising stunts run by the same people. Even in Heaven and Hell the same consortium seems to be in charge. Hell is just like any other town; no fire, devils, or interesting people sizzling on grids, the Ghost complains, and Heaven itself is "darned uncomfortable" (GD: 55). When Lewis suggests that Heaven might become more suitable if they stayed and let Heaven change them, the hardbitten Ghost finds this suggestion ridiculous.

> All this poppycock about growing harder so that the grass doesn't hurt your feet, now! There's an example. What would you say if you went to a hotel where the eggs were all bad; and when you complained to the Boss, instead of apologizing and changing his dairyman, he just told you that if you tried you'd get to like bad eggs in time? (GD: 56)

The cynical Ghost was correct; the outskirts of Heaven as Lewis imagined them were very unpleasant to the souls that arrived there. A single apple was too heavy to lift, and even the grass was sharp as knives and as hard as diamonds. Lewis wanted the landscape to convey his conviction that Heaven is reality itself, and reality can't change just to suit people who have their own ideas about what Heaven should be like.

The Goal of Sanctification

Lewis is quite definite about God's plan for the human race – nothing less than perfection. But how and when will he accomplish this? And what about the theological corner I mentioned in chapter three into which Lewis has painted himself? Here's how he got there. First, only Jesus was God in the flesh (the incarnation). Next, Jesus is the only human who lived a sinless life and so he is the only one who could offer himself as the perfect and final sacrifice for the sins of the world. Finally, only by Jesus dwelling within can believers have God's life in themselves. If Jesus is the only way to God's forgiveness and everlasting life, as Christianity has always claimed (it's not really Lewis's corner, after all), what will become of all those who never heard the good news? Lewis sets forth the solution in *The Great Divorce*.

Lewis often thought and wrote about the ultimate destiny of mankind. In his daily readings of the Bible, he encountered many passages about the final judgment. How could the sinful, imperfect, often deceived human race stand before the God whose holiness made him a "consuming fire" to sinners (Heb 12:29)? There was only one possible answer: perfection of the soul through Christ. Yes, there is forgiveness in Christ (justification), but the old nature still tries to have its way, often aided by the attempts of the enemy that Lewis wrote about in *The Screwtape Letters*. Justification is the doctrine that the righteousness of Christ is imputed or given by God to those who believe Christ died for their sins, and sanctification is the process by which God actually brings us in thought, word, and deed to the attainment of that righteousness.

In the 1984 movie *The Terminator*, Arnold Schwarzenegger plays a cyborg sent from the future to kill Sarah Connor because she will have a son that will help humans in the future defeat the machines that are taking over the world. Then Kyle Reese also arrives from the future to protect Sarah. Naturally, she doesn't understand what is happening at first, and tries to return to normal life after Kyle has helped her escape from the cyborg. "You don't understand," he tells her. "It's not human. It doesn't sleep, it won't stop, it will keep tracking you down until you are dead! That's what it does – it's a terminator!"

And that is exactly how Lewis views sanctification. God is holy, and he will track down every sin and terminate it. That's what he does. God says to each believer: "If you let me, I will make you perfect . . . whatever suffering it may cost you in your earthly life, whatever inconceivable purification it may cost you after death, whatever it costs Me, I will never rest, nor let you rest, until you are literally perfect" (MC: 158). Lewis shows here that he believed purification, that is, the process of sanctification, continued "after death." What did he mean?

Whereas some believers in the Protestant tradition teach that it is possible to be completely sanctified before death, Lewis did not hold this position, and the experience of most Christians supports his view. He concluded "the job will not be completed in this life; but He means to get us as far as possible before death" (MC: 159). The implications are clear: if all sin has not been removed before death, and God won't be satisfied until all sin has been cleansed, then the process must continue after we die. In other words, Lewis believed in Purgatory.

The Concept of Purgatory

The concept of Purgatory has been around for a very long time and for good reason: it explains when and how the process of sanctification continues after death. Over the centuries Purgatory acquired some negative connotations due to such abuses as the selling of indulgences, but these do not affect the theological importance of Purgatory. Lewis himself did not agree with the full Catholic understanding of Purgatory, but he did agree that the most important thing about Purgatory is not some *place* in the spirit world but the *purification* of the soul.

In sum, Lewis's conception of Purgatory is (keeping things simple) the completion or at least the continuation of the sanctification of the believer, and for most people, the process is not complete during this life. There are really only three possibilities: perfection through sanctification during our earthly life, at the time of physical death, or after death. This last option calls for caution; Scripture is not clear if perfection is reached during the intermediate state, or after the resurrection of the body when we stand before Christ. Perhaps both settings will have a part to play in the process of sanctification.

Only one option remains for most Protestants in regard to sanctification, since they agree with Lewis that perfection is unlikely in this life, and since they wish to avoid the Catholic doctrine of Purgatory. Physical death is the point of no return as far as salvation and spiritual progress is concerned. "The tree lies as it falls" is the metaphor Lewis uses to describe the Protestant position (GD: 69). And yet, can this view hold up to a closer look?

The strength of this position is that the emphasis is upon God as sanctifier, and its weakness is that it removes our participation. Some would argue that believers struggle with sin during their lives, they have prayed to have it removed, and now that life is over, God answers their prayers and cleanses the soul. But I think Lewis would respond by pointing out that when we accepted Christ and gave him permission to remove our sins in *this* world, *before* physical death, sanctification was neither immediate nor automatic.

The fault is not God's. Humans have a tendency to hang on to those sins that "so easily beset us," even after a profession of faith. Indeed, we are often not even aware of our sins until God reveals them to us. When he does reveal them to us, we may be unwilling to surrender them; to pay the price of their removal. Even when we are willing, he usually asks us to struggle with them (no doubt to grow in strength and also in reliance on him), instead of immediately removing them. Sanctification, then, requires our cooperation and participation, and so Lewis rejects the "at death" option. Reflecting on the loss of his wife, he wrote: "How do I know that all her anguish is past? I never believed before – I thought it immensely improbable – that the faithfulest soul could leap straight into perfection and peace the moment death has rattled in the throat" (GO: 35). The only option left is Purgatory.

A central aspect of Purgatory is that pain will be an integral part of the soul's experience there. Lewis accepts pain as part of sanctification, both before and after death, but the results make the pain worthwhile.

> I assume that the process of purification will normally involve suffering. Partly from tradition; partly because most real good that has been done me in this life has involved it. But I don't think suffering is the purpose of the purgation. I can well believe that people neither much worse nor much better than I will suffer less than I or more. "No nonsense about merit." The treatment given will be the one required, whether it hurts little or much.
>
> My favourite image on this matter comes from the dentist's chair. I hope that when the tooth of life is drawn and I am "coming round," a voice will say, "Rinse your mouth out with this." *This* will be Purgatory. The rinsing may take longer than I can now imagine. The taste of *this* may be more fiery and astringent than my present sensibility could endure. But More and Fisher [Catholic theologians who depicted Purgatory as a place of severe torment by devils] shall not persuade me that it will be disgusting and unhallowed. (LTM: 109)

But if the process is the crucial matter, the place of Purgatory is still important since it is part of the spirit world. In the Scriptures, Heaven is "up" and Hades is "down," but both are actually "places" in the same spirit world. Many of Lewis's ideas of the spirit world came from our physical world because he viewed this world and this life as "Shadow Lands," and the invisible spirit world as the eternal reality of which this existence is only a faint but real reflection.

> "The Eagle is right," said the Lord Digory. "Listen, Peter. When Aslan said you could never go back to Narnia, he meant the Narnia you were thinking of. But that was not the real Narnia. It had a beginning and an end. It was only a shadow or copy of

the real Narnia, which has always been here and always will be here: just as our own world, England and all, is only a shadow or copy of something in Aslan's real world. (LB: 169)

Plato and Scripture agree that our present world is only a reflection of more substantial realities we do not now see. Paul mentioned the "true Narnia" in 2 Corinthians 4:17–18, a text Lewis knew well since he took his famous sermon "The Weight of Glory" from this passage. "For this slight moment-ary affliction is preparing us for an eternal weight of glory beyond all measure, because we look not at what can be seen but at what cannot be seen; for what can be seen is temporary, but what cannot be seen is eternal."

So then Narnia is an imaginary version of the real and eternal Narnia, just as our world is of Heaven, or the spirit world. (I'm using the expression "spirit world" to contrast with the *physical* or material world in which we live. "Spirit" reminds us that this is where spirits like angels and God exist, and the spirit world includes all "places," such as Hades depicted in the Bible as "below" and Heaven "above.") And Lewis thought and wrote much about the spirit world because he knew that was the destiny of every human being and because the redemptive work of Jesus did not end on the cross but also continued in the spirit world and greatly changed things there.

The Descent of Christ in **The Great Divorce**

Let me explain. As an Anglican, Lewis would have been quite familiar with the Apostle's Creed, which includes the words "He [Jesus] descended into Hell." In church tradition, the descent of Christ and his releasing of captive humans so that they could ascend with him into Paradise came to be known as the "winnowing of Hell," though it is more accurate to refer to this part of the underworld as Hades (the Old Testament word is *sheol*) – an intermediate state between death and resurrection where change is still possible – than Hell, the final state of those who reject God. The importance of this part of Christ's redemption to Lewis is shown in that he included it prominently when he retold the gospel story. We've already seen the descent in *The Lion, the Witch and the Wardrobe*, when Aslan and the girls flew to the Witch's castle; and in *Perelandra*, when Ransom finally was able to end his struggle with the Unman by crushing his head with a rock and pushing his body over the edge of a cliff and down into a lake of fire. Now, in *The Great Divorce*, an imaginary trip to the spirit world after Christ has been there, Lewis gives his most developed treatment of Purgatory in his fictional works.

In *The Lion, the Witch and the Wardrobe*, Lewis emphasized the freeing of the stone captives held prisoner in the Hades of the Witch's castle, while in *Perelandra*, the struggle with Satan is the focus. But Lewis isn't finished. Inspired by the great poetry of Dante's *Comedia* (in English, *Divine Comedy*), which described a visit to Hell, Purgatory, and Paradise, Lewis makes the same trip, but this time on a bus! Just as Dante had his hero, Virgil (who also described a journey to the underworld), to serve as his "tour guide," so Lewis gives this honor to George MacDonald, the Scottish minister to whom Lewis owed so much, even saying that MacDonald's book *Phantastes* had "baptized" his imagination.

In *The Great Divorce*, Lewis dreams that he finds himself walking for hours in a run-down section of town. Rain is falling, and time seems frozen in twilight. The town seems empty until he finally comes to a bus stop where people are lined up. Quarrels break out as they wait, everyone shoves and pushes to get on when the bus arrives, and yet there seems to be room for all. As they leave the ground and travel across a huge abyss, Lewis speaks with various people on the bus; each of them seems to be nursing a grudge of some kind against someone else or God himself.

The bus ride ends in a beautiful, pastoral setting that gives the impression of enormous size. Once again, time seems to have stopped, but up here morning is just about to dawn. Everyone piles out of the bus with more pushing and shouting, leaving Lewis to exit last. He begins to enjoy the beauty around him, but finds everything immensely hard and solid. Even the blades of grass are as sharp and as hard as diamonds.

Soon he notices spirits approaching in the distance, and as they draw closer, Lewis can see they are as solid and heavy as the landscape. They have been changed and now belong to this place. Each of them seems to know one of the passengers that arrived on the bus, and they begin to speak with them, attempting to persuade them to confront the sins in their life, allow God to remove them, and then accompany them on the journey into Heaven. The bus has delivered them to the outskirts of Heaven, but now they need to go higher up and farther in.

The Theology of Purgatory in Seven Principles

Lewis has really unleashed his imagination, but the focus is obviously upon the end of the process of sanctification. Those who wish can always take the bus from the Grey Town to the outskirts of Heaven. Those who stay there will look back and say it was Purgatory, while to those who refuse Heaven, it will have been Hell. Since this is Lewis's most extensive and complex depiction of Purgatory, a closer look at the seven principles upon which *The Great Divorce* rests should clarify his theology of sanctification after death.

First principle: the soul does not "sleep" after physical death. Some Christians have taught that we become unconscious at death and do not regain consciousness until Christ returns. Lewis disagrees, and depicts each Ghost and Spirit in *The Great Divorce* as fully human in personality. Is he correct? Scripture reveals very little about human existence after physical death, but such passages as the parable of the Rich Man and Lazarus (Luke 16:19–31) and the souls of the martyrs under the altar (Rev 6:9–11) describe deceased humans as still having the essential qualities of the soul: consciousness, intellect, will, and emotions. Moral change is still possible; otherwise Purgatory serves no purpose. This does not imply that deceased humans are now complete, since they have been freed from their sinful bodies. God's redemptive plans for us include the resurrection of our physical bodies, and only then will we be complete and fully human.

Second principle: who and what we are is the result of all of our moral choices. Sanctification is impossible without the grace of God, but we also play a part. We can choose; indeed, we make many moral choices during our lives. "Every time you make a choice you are turning the central part of you . . . either into a Heavenly creature or into a Hellish creature" (MC: 72). The grumbling Ghost we meet in *The Great Divorce* is in danger of becoming only a grumble, explains MacDonald (GD: 74). This principle is an important antidote to the theology that stresses only the new birth of a believer to the neglect of spiritual development afterwards.

Third principle: God will not sanctify us unless we allow him to do so. The strongest example of this in *The Great Divorce* is the Angel who tells the man with the red lizard (it represents lust) on his shoulder: "I cannot kill it against your will. It is impossible. Have I your permission?" (GD: 99). Through his Spirit God convicts us of sin and through his grace he helps us conquer sin, but only if we acknowledge the sin he shows us and accept the grace he offers. I hasten to add that this principle does not imply believers can be passive in the process of sanctification; the second principle requires our involvement. Paul also reminds us that we have an active part to play: "Since we have these promises...let us purify ourselves from everything that contaminates body and spirit, perfecting holiness out of reverence for God" (2 Cor 7:1).

Lewis is quite aware that the credit for our spiritual progress must ultimately go to God. "I have been talking as if it were we who did everything. In reality, of course, it is God who does everything. We, at most, allow it to be done to us" (MC: 150). If we resist, God can convict us, woo us, reprimand us, and even punish us, but ultimately, as Lewis puts it, we finally yield to God and say, "Thy will be done," or we rebel until God finally says to us, "Thy will be done" (GD: 72).

Fourth principle: no sin can enter Heaven. Not even, insists Lewis, "the smallest and most intimate souvenirs of Hell" (GD: 10). Of course, sins don't have an independent existence; what this really means is that no *person*, whether pagan or Christian, can enjoy (endure?) eternal fellowship with God until every sin has been removed. God is utterly and completely holy, and only those who have put on the righteousness of Christ can have fellowship with him.

Fifth principle: "seek and you shall find." These familiar words come from the Sermon on the Mount and Lewis quoted them through MacDonald: "Those who seek find. To those who knock it is opened" (GD: 72). The complete text is: "Ask and you shall receive, seek and you shall find, knock and the door shall be opened to you. For everyone who asks receives, and everyone who searches finds, and for everyone who knocks the door will be opened" (Matthew 7:7–8). Lewis did not cheapen these words by viewing them as promises for wealth or perfect health, but as God's promise that anyone who sincerely desires God will find him. This principle pervades each dialogue in *The Great Divorce*, as the Spirits do everything in their power to persuade the Ghosts to relinquish their sins and embrace God's forgiveness. As MacDonald tells Lewis: "If there's one wee spark under all those ashes, we'll blow it till the whole pile is red and clear" (GD: 74).

Sixth principle: Lewis believed that "places" in the spirit world like Paradise and Hades were "timeless," or at least very different from the space-time continuum in which we experience life on the surface of our planet. This principle (perhaps I should say hypothesis) of Lewis explains why *The Great Divorce* contains expressions like "There is no other day. All days are present now" (GD: 98), "This moment contains all moments" (GD: 98), and "All moments that have been or shall be were, or are, present in the moment of His descending" (GD: 121).

Seventh principle: Jesus is the only way. In *Mere Christianity* Lewis identified Jesus as God incarnate, the sinless sacrifice for the sins of the world, and the one who gives divine life to us. Now Lewis adds in *The Great Divorce* that he is the only one who descended into the underworld (between his death and resurrection) to finish our sanctification.

The Descent of Christ in Scripture

Before I go any farther, I think I should give the scriptural basis for Christ's descent into the underworld. Many believers today have seldom if ever heard sermons or Sunday school lessons on this part of the redemptive work of Christ. In fact, some evangelical scholars began to attack this belief during the last half of the twentieth century for reasons that are still not clear to me. Therefore, I shall briefly explain why Christ descended, what happened when he did, and give the scriptural support for this interesting tenet of the faith.

To begin with, Jesus himself often spoke of returning to his Father in Heaven. And he also promised to make a change in the spirit world for his disciples: "In my Father's house there are many dwelling places. If it were not so, would I have told you that I go to prepare a place for you? And if I go and prepare a place for you, I will come again and will take you to myself, so that where I am, there you may be also" (John 14:2–3). "This presumably means that He is about to create that whole new Nature which will provide the environment or conditions for His glorified humanity and, in Him, for ours" (M: 154).

The Scriptures suggest (conclusive proof is difficult to find) that this new environment is called Paradise. The promise of Jesus to the thief on the cross who acknowledged him was, "Today you will be with me in Paradise" (Luke 23:43). And Paul tells the Corinthians that when he was caught up to the third Heaven, he was "caught up into Paradise and heard things that are not to be told, that no mortal is permitted to repeat" (2 Cor 12:4). (Note: in the Latin and Greek translations of the Old Testament, the Garden of Eden is called "Paradise." Perhaps the earthly Paradise was a reflection of the Paradise Christ has prepared in the spirit world.)

In his sermon on the Day of Pentecost, Peter told his listeners that the body of Jesus did not experience corruption in the grave, nor was his soul abandoned in Hades (Acts 2:25–31; a fulfillment of Psalm 16:10). Thus Jesus experienced death as a human being, but unlike us, he triumphed over both places. "I was dead, and see, I am alive forever and ever; and I have the keys of Death and of Hades" (Rev 1:18.) There are at least three Biblical passages that describe the effects of that triumph:

> Therefore it is said, "When he ascended on high he made captivity itself a captive; he gave gifts to his people." (When it says, "He ascended," what does it mean but that he had also descended into the lower parts of the earth? He who descended

is the same one who ascended far above all the Heavens, so that he might fill all things.) (Ephesians 4:8–10)

For Christ also suffered for sins once for all, the righteous for the unrighteous, in order to bring you to God. He was put to death in the flesh, but made alive in the spirit, in which also he went and made a proclamation to the spirits in prison, who in former times did not obey, when God waited patiently in the days of Noah, during the building of the ark, in which a few, that is, eight persons, were saved through water. (1 Peter 3:18–20)

For this is the reason the gospel was proclaimed even to the dead, so that, though they had been judged in the flesh as everyone is judged, they might live in the spirit as God does. (1 Peter 4:6)

Near the end of *The Great Divorce*, Lewis directly refers to the second passage when he has MacDonald say "there is no spirit in prison to whom He did not preach" (GD: 121). A minor correction is in order. Most scholars agree "spirits in prison" refers not to human souls as Lewis thought, but to the lustful angels that came down in Noah's time, married human women, taught mankind many dangerous skills, and so corrupted the world that God wiped it out by a flood (Gen 6:1–7, and many intertestamental Jewish sources such as 1 Enoch). Peter returns to this theme in his second epistle and tells us that they are imprisoned in Tartarus, the lowest section of Hades in ancient mythology. Peter likely meant that Christ told them that their attempts to corrupt the human race by intermarriage and so prevent the birth of the promised redeemer had failed.

At any rate, the third passage does refer to human souls. Now Peter clearly states that Jesus went to Hades to proclaim the gospel to deceased humans. Some modern translations read "even to those who are *now* dead," but the word "now" is not in the Greek text. Combining all the texts,

Christ's journey to Hades took him first to the lowest part where the angels were and are still imprisoned. Then, moving "upward" and "leading captivity captive," he freed the human souls from Hades who were willing to go with him and brought them into Paradise, the place he prepared for them. Next, the resurrection brought Jesus once again into time and space as we know them, and Luke tells us he met with his disciples for a period of forty days, teaching them about the kingdom of God (Acts 1:3). Then he ascended into Heaven as they watched, took his place at the right hand of God, and finally sent the Holy Spirit on the Day of Pentecost, the event that gave birth to the church.

When I describe the descent of Christ into Hades in class, my students often point out that in the parable of the Rich Man and Lazarus, no one was able to pass from one compartment of Hades to the other, because a vast gulf divided them (Luke 16:26). Lewis was quite aware of this; in fact, he refers to that gulf as a "radiant abyss" in *The Great Divorce*. But Lewis would see the "geography" of the parable as the Biblical way of teaching about spiritual conditions more than about literal places. Whether literal or not, the real challenge is to somehow bridge the chasm that separates shrunken human souls from God. And so, MacDonald tells Lewis, "Only the Greatest of all can make Himself small enough to enter Hell. For the higher a thing is, the lower it can descend – a man can sympathize with a horse but a horse cannot sympathize with a rat. Only one has descended into Hell" (GD: 121).

Returning to the first passage, when Paul describes Christ's descent in Ephesians 4:9–10, he writes: "when he ascended...he led captives in his train." In other words, some souls did leave the underworld and ascended with Christ, probably to Paradise, or the "outskirts" of Heaven; the setting in which Lewis places most of *The Great Divorce*. But who left with Christ? Only those who wanted to, who were willing to embrace Truth himself, Lewis would answer. Perhaps Jesus was speaking to the Pharisees about his descent, before it happened in time, but already known in the eternal present, when he told them that Abraham, whom they respected so highly, not only wanted to know about Christ, but had indeed seen "my day" and rejoiced at what he saw (John 8:56).

And, I might add, those who went with Christ to Paradise shall again accompany him when he returns. As Paul reminds the Thessalonians, "God will bring with Jesus those who have fallen asleep [died] in him" (1 Thess 4:14). Thus there is Biblical support, both direct and indirect, for the historical Christian belief in the descent of Christ to the underworld and for some of the dead leaving their chambers in Hades and ascending with Christ to Paradise.

Applying the Seven Principles

These seven principles are, I believe, the key concepts underlying the theology expressed by Lewis in *The Great Divorce*, and he arrived at them from his understanding of the Scriptures. But how can they all be true when on the one hand, God wants everyone to be saved, and yet the path to God is only through Jesus, whose existence is unknown to billions of humans? Let's begin on one side of the problem: how does God feel about our salvation?

Will all be saved?

There are Biblical passages that seem to indicate that some are chosen by God to know him, which implies others are not. Other passages like John 3:16 include everyone: "God so loved the world" and "whoever believes in Him might have eternal life." Lewis prefers the more inclusive approach, since it agrees with the promise of Jesus that whoever seeks will surely find. More support comes from such passages as 1 Timothy 2:4, which states that God "desires *everyone* to be saved and to come to the knowledge of the truth;" and 2 Peter 3:9: God "is patient with you, *not wanting any to perish*, but *all* to come to repentance."

When we add the omnipotence of God to this view of salvation, the implication is that all will be saved; this is the doctrine known as universalism. The logic behind this position is as follows: God wishes all to be saved, as the Bible affirms, and if he is all-powerful, and all-knowing, then he is able to achieve this (and any other) purpose that is consistent with his nature. Almost since the beginning of Christianity some believers have understood God's love for us in this way. Carried to the extreme, a few have even concluded that Satan will some day return to God.

Universalism is an attractive belief. Who wouldn't rejoice at the prospect of an empty Hell, a defeated Satan without a single human captive after all his efforts, and all humanity finally free of sin and giving glory to God? God knows what is best for us, so why shouldn't he overrule our sinful "no" to him, and lead us to salvation against our will, knowing that once we have received salvation and the spiritual sight that comes with it, we will thank God for overcoming our defiance?

Indeed, Lewis's own conversion was precisely along these lines. In *Surprised by Joy* he describes God's grace in his life in terms of the parable of the Great Banquet, in which the master looking for dinner guests instructed his servant to go out into the streets and "compel them to come in" (Luke 14:23). And so the grace of God transformed the "most dejected and reluctant convert in all England" (SBJ: 228–9) into an apologist for the faith! If God did this for Lewis, why not the same for every person? Indeed, even George MacDonald, Lewis's tour guide in *The Great Divorce*, was reputed to be a universalist (GD: 121).

But the Bible checks us at this point. It teaches that some will be lost, including the antichrist and the false prophet who attempt to rule the world at the end of the age, and lost forever (Rev 20:15). And if perdition will be the final state of some, this can mean only one thing. When the will and the omnipotence of God encounter human choice, God respects our choices rather than force salvation upon the beings he has created with a will separate from his own. Perhaps a case could be made for the use of divine force, the bitter medicine that is the only cure for a fatal illness, but Lewis sees things differently.

> In creating beings with free will, omnipotence from the outset submits to the possibility of such defeat. What you call defeat, I call miracle: for to make things which are not Itself, and thus to become, in a sense, capable of being resisted by its own handi-work, *is the most astonishing and unimaginable of all the feats we attribute to the Deity*. (PP: 127)

The result is rather paradoxical when we express it from this perspective: rather than God *sending* sinners to Hell (or perhaps even worse, forcing them into Heaven), he finally yields to *their own choice*. Lewis even goes so far as to describe Hell as an expression of God's mercy, since it is part of his creation and the most suitable place for those who refuse Heaven. "God in his mercy made the fixed pains of Hell" ("Divine Justice" in P: 98). And so Lewis (reluctantly?) parted ways with his mentor and tour guide George MacDonald on this point because he believed Heaven will be too painful for some who will not unveil.

The second principle also supports the position that physical death is not the final deciding point. A person of only thirty or forty years of age may already be beyond the reach of God, having rejected the work of the Holy Spirit in his life until he is no longer capable of responding to God. The tender heart of

Lucy had compassion for the Dwarfs, but even Aslan was unable to reach them in the prison they had built for themselves before they died. They are like those who refuse the bus ride in *The Great Divorce*: ''First they will not, in the end they cannot open their hands for gifts, or their mouths for food, or their eyes to see'' (GD: 121).

> But though freedom is real it is not infinite. Every choice reduces a little one's freedom to choose the next time. There therefore comes a time when the creature is fully *built*, irrevocably attached either to God or to itself. This irrevocableness is what we call Heaven or Hell. Every conscious agent is finally committed in the long run: i.e. it rises above freedom into willed, but henceforth unalterable, union with God, or else sinks below freedom into the black fire of self-imprisonment. (CLII: 585; ''To Joyce Pearce, July 20, 1943)

On the other hand, billions of people have died without ever hearing the gospel. The strength of Lewis's position is that the same principle of choice still applies; how did they respond to the truth as they were able to understand it in their own religion, or in the evidence of a Creator as expressed in nature and the conscience? Only God knows if they will still be open to the truth when they encounter it after death in Christ, but if they are, God will reach them because he is not willing that any should perish.

Is there a second chance?

When my students begin to understand Purgatory as Lewis explains it, they raise two objections. Why should people who heard the message while alive but then ignored or rejected it have a second chance? And if those who never knew that Christ died for their sins still can be saved, doesn't this rob the Great Commission of its urgency? Taking the second objection first, nothing can rob the gospel of its urgency. The sooner people believe the better. The older we get, Screwtape would remind us, the more comfortable we feel in this world. Surrendering to Another becomes increasingly difficult as habits become set. Also, the Christian life is not just a "fire escape" but an opportunity to be a transforming influence in the world. Besides, Jesus told us to go into all the world with the gospel; no concept of the afterlife can change that command.

But what about non-believers, and the possibility of a "second chance"? For those who have never heard, Purgatory would be a "first chance." And why is a second chance so objectionable? The fact of the matter is that many who live in countries where the gospel can be openly shared have had many chances to believe. I myself am the product of a second chance; I rejected the message of the first person who brought me the good news of salvation. Divine providence gives us all many chances as we encounter truth in various forms throughout life. Saved at the time of death or not, we choose until we have "fully built" ourselves, with God's grace, or without.

Beyond space and time

But when did Christ enter Hades to preach to the dead? When Lewis asks, "And will he ever do so again?" MacDonald's reply (speaking for Lewis) is astonishing: "It was not once long ago that He did it. Time does not work that way when once ye have left the Earth. All moments that have been or shall be were, or are, present in the moment of His descending. There is no spirit in prison to whom He did not preach" (GD: 121). In God's "unbounded Now" (Lewis's expression in Letter 27 of SL: 128), they meet Jesus. How they respond to Truth himself brings them closer and closer to the Eternal, or increases the

separation. By opening Purgatory to all with the sixth principle, Lewis disagrees with the Catholic view that only those
who will eventually go to Heaven first pass through Purgatory.

This concept of Purgatory also provides the way out of the
theological corner that has caused so many to struggle with
Christianity. Jesus is still the only way, but now everyone has
a chance to accept him; not just those who were fortunate
enough to live at the right place and time. Lewis upholds
the justice of God; now no one can say "I never heard."
The implications of this are so far-reaching they include all
humanity. For that reason, *The Great Divorce* may be more
theologically important than anything else Lewis wrote.

The stress Lewis placed upon the importance of the choices
made by the Ghosts should satisfy those who question the
justice and mercy of God. Since we are the product of all of
our moral choices, Lewis concludes that we choose our own
destiny. God doesn't gleefully send sinners to Hell, he grants
their wishes and only with reluctance. This seems contrary to
the way many people imagine God's judgment, but Lewis has
Scripture to support him. God declared his feelings in this
matter long ago through Ezekiel: "I take no pleasure in the
death of the wicked" (Eze 33:11). God is not willing that any
should perish, but he will not force people into Heaven. Lewis
rightfully concludes that Hell is the place God has mercifully
created for those who would rather escape reality.

Responding to truth

At this point, one might ask: "If everyone does have the
opportunity to choose or reject Christ after death, who
would not choose Heaven over Hell, now that spiritual issues
are so much clearer?" Who indeed would refuse to leave
Hades and ascend with Christ to Paradise? Well, Lewis shows
in every dialogue and even in the landscape of *The Great*

Divorce what sort of people would reject Heaven. Napoleon is pacing the floor and blaming everyone else for his problems. The Episcopal Ghost would rather discuss theology than exchange it for Truth himself. A poet refuses Heaven when he learns he has been forgotten on earth. A mother demands her son back from God whom she blames for his premature death. They all refuse to allow God to make them "solid" by killing what needs to die.

But Lewis won't budge; even the smallest sin causes *The Great Divorce* between Heaven and Hell. The reality of Heaven is too "big" to enter the shrunken, tightly closed souls of the Grey Town, and the glories of Heaven are unbearable to those who flee from the truth. Yet even in the Grey Town, God's reality can't be avoided. The souls there are able to construct houses simply by thinking of them, a symbol of the facades humans erect (or the veil they put on) to hide from others and from God. But the rain that never stops comes right through the houses, serving as a constant reminder of the futility of escaping reality.

Those who do take the bus ride, who begin to respond to the preaching of Christ in Hades, experience more suffering as they see themselves more clearly. During the ride, the bus expands as it leaves the shrunken edge of Hell and enters the edge of Heaven. The passengers are (spiritually) stretched so thin they are like transparent bubbles when they leave the bus. Now reality is truly overpowering. The grass is painfully sharp to walk on and Lewis nearly panics when the hardbitten Ghost reminds him that should it rain, every drop would go right through him like a bullet (GD: 57).

The Spirits who come to help the Ghosts are also terrifying, due to their solidity and Heavenly appearance. Things come to a crisis when the Spirits confront the Ghosts with their faults, even though they do so with gentle firmness in the service of Heaven. The Spirits were friends or family or associates down on earth; if Christ himself came, Lewis implies, the terror would overwhelm the Ghosts. Sure enough, at the very end of the book, the coming of Christ (who is ultimate reality) is heralded by rays of light so real they are like solid blocks of stone (GD: 125). Then, it is too late; the bus stop is closed. Night comes down below, and dawn finally breaks above. Lewis screams, for he is also a Ghost, and awakes from his dream.

The logical application of the seven principles brings Lewis to the conclusion that how a person responds to the truth *as he is able to understand it,* even if he has never heard the gospel message, is the most important part anyone can play in the process of sanctification. Some of my more hard-nosed students object to this, saying "you're either right or wrong, and if you're wrong God will send you to Hell!" And yet some of those same students listen to the lectures with attentive minds and sincere hearts, but arrive at different conclusions and even misunderstandings because they are not able to grasp accurately everything they hear. Will God "grade" us according to how much we were able to understand about him, or according to the condition of our heart? Lewis emphatically chooses the latter: what *more* can anyone do than embrace the truth as best as he can understand it? In fact, having a heart that longs for and welcomes the truth is even more important than how much the mind can grasp. Paul agrees, for he writes that we will be judged according to the intentions of our hearts (1 Cor 4:5), not by some IQ test that measures our understanding of theology.

Lewis emphasizes the importance of a sincere heart quite dramatically in *The Last Battle* through the figure of Emeth, whose name is Hebrew for faithfulness and *truth.* Emeth had been serving Tash, the Satan-like, chief god of the Calormenes, because he had been deceived by someone he trusted. His heart was sincere in his search for truth, yet he was completely wrong in his choices. When he finally meets Aslan, Emeth is greatly discouraged and waits for Aslan to pronounce his condemnation. But Aslan tells him "all the service thou hast done to Tash, I account as service done to me ... Beloved ... unless thy desire had been for me thou wouldst not have sought so long and so truly. For all find what they truly seek" (LB: 165–6).

Emeth represents for Lewis the "virtuous unbeliever" ("Letter to Patricia Thomson" in L: 362, December 8, 1941) who wanted to serve God and thought he was doing so. Untold millions have been utterly deceived as Emeth was, and/or limited by their cultural contexts, religions, and leaders. Is there any hope for them? Lewis believed so because the parable of the Sheep and the Goats (Matt 25:31–46) left that door open. In that parable, Jesus welcomes into eternal life those Gentiles who served him by helping others in need. They seem confused, as if they are meeting Jesus for the first time, and ask how they helped him. Jesus explains, "As you did it to one of the least of these who are members of my family, you did it to me" (Matt 25:40). Lewis mentioned this parable at least eight times, and its more generous view of salvation clearly fascinated him.

> I think that every prayer which is sincerely made even to a false god or to a very imperfectly conceived true God, is accepted by the true God and that Christ saves many who do not think they know Him. For He is (dimly) present in the *good* side of the inferior teachers they follow. In the parable of the Sheep and the Goats ... those who are saved do not seem to know that they have served Christ. ("Letter to Miss Ashton" in L: 428, November 8, 1952)

Lewis did not restrict the parable to our prayers: "Looking at the Sheep & Goats every man can be quite sure that every kind act he does will be accepted by Christ" ("Letter to Emily

McLay" in L: 433, August 3, 1953). But Lewis saw a problem in this emphasis upon our actions. In the same letter he admits he is unable to reconcile the "salvation by works" theology of the parable with Paul's theology of salvation by faith. The answer Lewis was searching for comes in the epistle of James, who understands works as the expression of true faith.

How does this theology of the "virtuous unbeliever" interface with the seven principles Lewis used to form his concept of Purgatory? The parable does suggest a broader understanding of how everyone will find salvation through Christ, even those who did not know him during their earthly lives. But principle four remains in full force: all sin must be removed – not just forgiven – and new life given to all, before fellowship with a holy God is possible. The approving words of Jesus in the parable suggest that the commendable deeds of those who helped others in need shaped their souls so that they were receptive to Jesus when they finally did stand before him, and allowed him to prepare them for Heaven.

Purgatory in Scripture

Does the Bible really support the concept of Purgatory? The answer is "no," if one is looking for the word "Purgatory" or a passage directly dealing with this belief. But Purgatory as Lewis defined it – moral/spiritual change (for the better) after death – does have Biblical support. Hebrews 11, the well-known "Bible hall of fame," describes a number of people from Old Testament times who "through faith" accomplished many great feats. But the last two verses of this chapter tell us that although they lived and died in faith, they did not receive what they had been promised. Why? Because "God had planned something better for us so that only together with us *would they be made perfect*" (Heb 11:40). The whole message of Hebrews is that the "something better" is salvation through Christ. Because they lived before Christ, they died without his salvation. Yet the author anticipates their salvation; indeed, their perfection. Since they have already died, their perfection is only possible through a post-death encounter with Christ.

Have they been perfected? In the next chapter, the author gives us a glimpse of the spirit world and they are there, having finally received what their faith anticipated:

> But you have come to Mount Zion and to the city of the living God, the Heavenly Jerusalem, and to innumerable angels in festal gathering, and to the assembly of the firstborn who are enrolled in Heaven, and to God the judge of all, *and to the spirits of the righteous made perfect*, and to Jesus, the mediator of a new covenant, and to the sprinkled blood that speaks a better word than the blood of Abel. (Heb 12:22–24)

Summary

Now the full force of the implications of Christ's descent as Lewis understands it becomes clear. Since the descent is an event beyond time as we know it, everyone who has ever lived reaches the underworld at the same "time." There, Christ invites everyone, Christian or not, to leave Hades and journey with him to Paradise; i.e., to embrace the truth, accept God's forgiveness, and enter into fellowship with God. Here (and at the cross) is the ultimate expression of "God so loved the world" and "God is not willing that any should perish."

The seven principles of Purgatory not only vindicate the justice of God, they allow those who have chosen Heaven to experience fullness of joy. Why? Because they will understand that no one went to Hell simply because they never heard the good news. Only those who demand Hell go there. As MacDonald explains it to Lewis: "Either the day must come when joy prevails and all the makers of misery are no longer able to infect it: or else for ever and ever the makers of misery can destroy in others the happiness they reject for themselves" (GD: 118). The self-imprisoned will not be able to "blackmail the universe" (GD: 118).

Finally, we also find here the resolution to the problem of attempting to reconcile such statements as "No one comes to the Father except through me" (John 14:6) and "There is no other name under Heaven...by which we must be saved" (Acts 4:12), with the reality that untold millions have never heard the gospel. Everyone, believer and unbeliever alike, will encounter Christ after death, and everyone must choose or reject the truth until conformed to the image of Christ, or until they have become a person beyond the reach of even the grace of God. The issue for Lewis is not a "second chance," but the grace of God responding to a lifetime (and beyond) of choices. God is able to complete the process of sanctification. He will settle for nothing less.

Chapter 7

God's Plan for the Body – and the Universe

''The judgment of Narnia.''
Illustration © 2007 by Deborah Wilson Camp

"Further in and higher up!"

(LB: 154)

But as they came right up to Aslan one or other of two things happened to each of them. They all looked straight *in his face*; *I don't think they had any choice about that*. And when some looked, the expression of their faces changed terribly – it was fear and hatred; except that, on the faces of Talking Beasts, the fear and hatred lasted only for a fraction of a second. You could see that they suddenly ceased to be *Talking* Beasts. They were just ordinary animals. And all the creatures who looked at Aslan that way swerved to their right, his left, and disappeared into his huge black shadow, which (as you have heard) streamed away to the left of the doorway. The children never saw them again. I don't know what became of them. But the others looked *in the face of Aslan* and loved him, though some of them were very frightened at the same time.

(LB: 153–4, emphasis mine)

Resurrection of the Body

Before we come to the consummation of God's redemptive work, let's review briefly. Lewis believed that as God in the flesh, Jesus offered up his sinless life on the cross as payment for the sins of the world. When a person acknowledges his sinfulness and accepts salvation through Christ, the journey to perfection (sanctification) begins. It continues, Lewis believed, after death when Jesus himself entered Hades and brought out to Paradise those who believe in him. And then, something happened never before seen "in the whole history of the universe ... He has forced open a door that has been locked since the death of the first man. He has met, fought, and beaten the King of Death. Everything is different because He has done so. This is the beginning of the New Creation: a new chapter in cosmic history has opened" (M: 150).

But God isn't finished with us amphibians yet. We've considered the changes of the soul in this life and beyond, but what about our bodies? The redemptive work of Christ, as Paul reminded the Corinthians (1 Cor 15), includes the physical body also, so we must not regard it as unimportant. Lewis had a well-developed theology of the future, and believed all of creation, not just our bodies, would be transformed by God. In the same context as the resurrection Lewis also anticipated the last judgment, when sheep would finally be separated from goats (Matt 25:31–46, the parable he often cited), glory or shame revealed, and sin finally exposed and forever banished. Lewis summarized the predictions of the Bible for believers in these five promises:

> The promises of Scripture may very roughly be reduced to five heads. It is promised (1) that we shall be with Christ; (2) that we shall be like Him; (3) with an enormous wealth of imagery, that we shall have "glory"; (4) that we shall, in some sense, be fed or feasted or entertained; and (5) that we shall have some sort of official position in the universe – ruling cities, judging angels, being pillars of God's temple. ("Weight of Glory" in WG: 34)

The promise of becoming "like Him" must include the resurrection of the body, because Jesus has a resurrected body. What might become of the physical body when the promise of the resurrection finally comes to pass? Lewis immediately lays aside any possibility of the corpse, long since reused by nature, somehow being brought back into service. St. Paul did not mean that, he adds (LTM: 121), which shows us that Lewis is referring to Paul's description of the resurrection in 1 Corinthians 15. There, Paul defends the belief in a literal resurrection, but also explains that what will be raised up will not be the same kind of body. "It is sown a physical body, it is raised a spiritual body" (1 Cor 15:44).

This "spiritual" body will be immortal, but what will it actually be like? Paul doesn't really get into that, other than saying the resurrection body will "bear the image of the man of Heaven" (meaning Jesus, 1 Cor 15:49). Lewis believed resurrected humanity will once again be able to participate in the material creation even as Jesus did, and so he concluded: "What the soul cries out for is the resurrection of the senses. Even in this life matter would be nothing to us if it were not the source of sensations" (LTM: 122).

Resurrection and Creation

Lewis believed this sensuous life of the resurrection body will be clothed by the soul, whereas in this natural life, the soul is clothed by the body. Yet even in our natural life, Lewis sees glimpses of what resurrection life might be like.

> At present, if we are reborn in Christ, the spirit in us lives directly on God; but the mind, and, still more, the body receives life from Him at a thousand removes – through our ancestors, through our food, through the elements. The faint, far-off results of those energies which God's creative rapture implanted in matter when He made the worlds are what we now call physical pleasures; and even thus filtered, they are too much for our present management. What would it be to taste at the fountainhead that stream of which even these lower reaches prove so intoxicating? Yet that, I believe, is what lies before us. The whole man is to drink joy from the fountain of joy. As St. Augustine said, the rapture of the saved soul will "flow over" into the glorified body. ("Weight of Glory" in WG: 44)

In that new sphere of existence where the senses have been restored to us in the glorified body, the world of matter in which we once lived will become a much richer part of our new life. In fact, Lewis predicts, God will accomplish this enhancement of nature *through* us. What we perceived and knew by the physical senses during our earthly life "became soul. That element in the soul which it becomes will, in my view, be raised and glorified; the hills and valleys of Heaven will be to those you now experience not as a copy is to an original, nor as a substitute is to the genuine article, but as the flower to the root, or the diamond to the coal" (LTM: 123).

> Then the new earth and sky, the same yet not the same as these, will rise in us as we have risen in Christ. And once again, after who knows what aeons of the silence and the dark, the birds will sing and the waters flow, and lights and shadows move across the hills, and the faces of our friends laugh upon us with amazed recognition. Guesses, of course, only guesses. If they are not true, something better will be. For "we know that we shall be made like Him, for we shall see Him as He is." (LTM: 124. Lewis is quoting 1 John 3:2, but he changes the text from "we shall be like Him" to "we shall be *made* like Him," no doubt wishing to emphasize God's power that will change us.)

The "new earth" even includes animals (at least some of them) because they are a part of nature and they have been taken up into us even more intimately than inanimate matter, as we discussed in chapter four.

> My stuff about animals came long ago in *The Problem of Pain*. I ventured the supposal – it could be nothing more – that as we are raised *in* Christ, so at least some animals are raised *in* us. Who knows, indeed, but that a great deal even of the inanimate creation is raised *in* the redeemed souls who have, during this life, taken its beauty into themselves? That may be the way in which the "new Heaven and the new earth" are formed. (LAL: 107, November 26, 1962)

The personality of tame animals is "largely the gift of man" (PP: 141). If we humans are raised to immortal life by Christ and our relationship is defined by such Biblical expressions as "in Christ" and "Christ in you the hope of glory," then by analogy, Lewis concludes, animals who become fully themselves "in us" may likewise share "in us" our new resurrection life. "As our mere soulhood is reborn to spirituality in Christ," so "their mere sentience is reborn to soulhood" (PP: 141).

Lewis means that when the quasi-spiritual and emotional value which human tradition attributes to a beast (such as the "innocence" of the lamb or the heraldic royalty of the lion) has a real ground in the beast's nature, and is not merely arbitrary or accidental, then it is in that capacity, or principally in that, that the beast may be expected to attend on risen man and follow after him as part of his "train" (PP: 141–2).

Just how deeply Lewis felt about the future of animals is revealed in a very moving description of one of the Spirits near the end of *The Great Divorce*. Lewis marvels at a woman of indescribable beauty. On earth, she was a nobody, and yet now "she is one of the great ones." MacDonald tells him: "Ye have heard that fame in this country and fame on Earth are two quite different things" (GD: 105). Following the woman, Sarah Smith of Golders Green, is a train of people and dozens of animals. MacDonald explains:

> "Every beast and bird that came near her had its place in her
> love. In her they became themselves. And now the abundance
> of life she has in Christ from the Father flows over into them."
> I looked at my Teacher in amazement.
> "Yes," he said. "It is like when you throw a stone into a pool,
> and the concentric waves spread out further and further. Who
> knows where it will end? Redeemed humanity is still young,
> it has hardly come to its full strength. But already there is

> joy enough in the little finger of a great saint such as yonder
> lady to waken all the dead things of the universe into life."
> (GD: 106–7)

Where is Lewis getting these amazing ideas? He has combined several Scriptures to form a vision of the new age. To the second promise ("We shall be like Him," taken from 1 John 3:2) he has added the miracles Jesus performed. Some of his miracles, such as turning water into wine (John 2:1–11) and feeding large crowds by multiplying loaves of bread and fish (Matt 15:32–39), reveal what God does every year in nature. But other miracles have a prophetic significance because they foretell what God will one day do universally. Next, Lewis brings Romans 8:18–25 into the discussion, which suggests our resurrection and glorification will be the means by which all creation shall be "set free from its bondage to decay."

> He raised one man ... from the dead because He will one day
> raise all men from the dead. Perhaps not only men, for there are
> hints in the New Testament that all creation will eventually be
> rescued from decay, restored to shape and subserve the splen-
> dour of re-made humanity. The Transfiguration and the walk-
> ing on the water are glimpses of the beauty and the effortless
> power over all matter which will belong to men when they are
> really waked by God. ("Miracles" in GID: 32–3)

Even now, and since the worlds were spoken into existence, Jesus is the One in whom "all things hold together" (Col 1:17). Now warped by sin (which began in Heaven with the angels, not on earth), the universe may be more difficult than before to "manage," just as our fallen world requires more effort from us. But all creation will be redeemed, set free from decay, including us, and since God gives us dignity through meaningful work for him, Lewis expects that resurrected and glorified humanity will participate in that liberation.

Judgment by Fire

The Ghosts in *The Great Divorce* were assisted in the process of sanctification by the Spirits who came to help them see themselves more honestly, confess their faults, and let God remove them. When a Ghost allowed that to happen, upward progress into the heights of Heaven soon removed him from Lewis's sight. But Lewis knew that sanctification and glorification didn't end in Purgatory; what happens there is meant to prepare us to stand before Christ. "He shall come again to judge the quick and the dead," reads the Nicene Creed, and Lewis took these words to mean the last day will reveal what we really are.

> It will be infallible judgment. If it is favorable we shall have no fear, if unfavorable, no hope that it is wrong. We shall not only believe, we shall know, know beyond doubt in every fibre of our appalled or delighted being, that as the Judge has said, so we are: neither more nor less nor other. We shall perhaps even realize that in some dim fashion we could have known it all along. ("The World's Last Night" in WLN: 113)

Not only will that scrutiny reveal what we truly are, it will also change us, if there still is need, and our sanctification will finally be complete. Here is where Lewis's first two promises come together. "We shall be with Him" is now completely true when we stand in his presence, and "We shall be like Him" will be the result. John made this connection in his first epistle: "Beloved, we are God's children now; what we will be has not yet been revealed. What we do know is this: when he is revealed, we will be like him, because we will see him as he is" (1 John 3:2).

Lewis wisely did not attempt to describe this encounter, but he did give us a preview of it in *The Great Divorce*. The man with a red lizard on his shoulder that symbolized lust is the only one in the dream who surrendered to God; the rest found the divine presence too painful. God's instrument in this case was an angel and Lewis reveals what sanctification involves through his description of the angel. He is so bright that Lewis can hardly look at him, as bright as "the morning sun at the beginning of a tyrannous summer day" (GD: 97). Heat as well as light flow out from the angel, for the glory of God is experienced as fire where sin is present and as light when sin is removed.

Eager to help, the angel approaches the man, who reacts with terror "You're burning me!" The lizard on the man's shoulder pleads with him to let it survive, but finally, the man gives the angel his consent. There is a horrible scream when the lizard is killed, but soon the man rises from the ground and stands beside the beautiful horse that appeared when lust was done away with. The warped love that is lust has been transformed by God into pure love and now instead of riding on the man, that love is a vehicle for him to ride into the heights of Heaven.

> The man turned from it [the horse], flung himself at the feet of the Burning One, and embraced them. When he rose I thought his face shone with tears, but it may have been only the liquid love and brightness (one cannot distinguish them in that country) which flowed from him...In joyous haste the young man leaped upon the horse's back...They were off before I well knew what was happening. There was riding if you like! I came out as quickly as I could from among the bushes to follow them with my eyes; but already they were only like a shooting star far off on the green plain, and soon among the foothills of the mountains. (GD: 100–1)

The parable of the Rich Man and Lazarus gives us a similar glimpse of Hades, although Paradise is not yet in view. The rich man asks Abraham to send Lazarus over to him with some water for his tongue because "I am in agony in these flames" (Luke 16:24). The story ends without revealing how he will respond when Jesus descends to Hades, but at least he is more aware of his condition than he was during his life when he feasted every day while ignoring Lazarus who was begging for food at his gate. Hopefully, as embarrassment, shame, and regret over his selfish life burn in his soul like fire, he will still be able to yield when Truth himself comes there.

Lewis chose the metaphor of fire because he understood that the glory of God would appear as light to the pure, but as fire wherever sin was still present. When Wormwood's patient was killed in the war, God appeared to him as "cool light," but to Wormwood that same glory was "blinding, suffocating fire" (SL: 148). As usual, Lewis is basing his descriptions on the Scriptures, which tell us "Our God is a consuming fire" (Heb 12:29), and he makes his angels "a flame of fire" (Heb 1:7), as the lustful man discovered.

Jesus himself said that everyone "will be salted with fire" (Mark 9:49). God intends for his fire to begin its work now, when believers are baptized with the Holy Spirit and fire (Matt 3:11). Sanctification continues in Hades as we move closer to God in Paradise, and reaches its climax when we stand before God. Paul tells us that "all of us must appear before the judgment seat of Christ" (2 Cor 5:10), and when we do,

> The work of each builder will become visible, for the Day will disclose it, because it will be revealed with fire, and the fire will test what sort of work each has done. If what has been built on the foundation survives, the builder will receive a reward. If the work is burned up, the builder will suffer loss; the builder will be saved, but only as through fire. (1 Cor 3:13–15)

The Face of God

Lewis has yet another perspective on our sanctification and the ultimate destination of mankind. Wormwood's patient saw "Him," meaning God himself, and Lewis believes that when the fire of God's glory has cleansed us, we shall see his face. The connection between God's glory and God's face is first revealed in the Scriptures when Moses is up on Mount Sinai. When God tells Moses that he has found favor with him, Moses makes the best of the positive situation and asks God to show him his glory. God's answer is quite revealing: "I will make all my goodness pass before you, and will proclaim before you the name, 'The lord'; and I will be gracious to whom I will be gracious, and will show mercy on whom I will show mercy. But," he said, "you cannot see my face; for no one shall see me and live" (Exo 33:19–20). Even so, God did let Moses see his back and just that exposure caused his face to shine so much that the Israelites were afraid of him (Exo 34:29–35). Moses had to wear a veil until the glory subsided; one day, our resurrection bodies will be able to reflect that glory much longer.

Why can't Moses – who found favor with God and spoke with him face to face (meaning not in dreams or visions) – see God's face? No one, God says, can see his face/glory and survive. Why not? Surely the answer is that the full glory of God would be fatal to us in our present condition. How ironic that our ultimate destination, the face (= presence, the glory) of God, to be our highest joy, would be fatal to us in our present condition. The occasional glimpses of that glory confirm God's refusal to Moses. In the transfiguration, Jesus's face became brighter than the sun (Matt 17:2). The same description – brighter than the sun – is used when Saul encounters Christ on the Damascus road (Acts 26:13).

Does God have an actual face or this is another example of attributing human features to God (anthropomorphic speech)? Theologians don't agree, but I will observe that just as we focus on the face to identify a person because the personality within is expressed there more than anywhere else in the body, so the divine glory evidently has a focal point.

The experiences of Moses and Saul should remind us that even in our mortal bodies we are able to endure a fleeting glimpse of God's glory, no doubt "reduced" for our sakes. And in a figurative sense, when we yield ourselves to God we are "seeing" him, if only dimly. In our new bodies, Paul tells us, we will see God face to face, just as Moses desired. But now, we must be satisfied to see God "through a mirror, in an enigma," as the Greek literally says (1 Cor 13:12).

And yet, even that indirect contact will enable God to sanctify us. In another mirror passage, Paul recalls the veil Moses had to wear. In contrast to the Israelites who did not want to see God's glory on the face of Moses, when people turn to God the veil is removed. Paul means that when we are open, honest, and sincere with God, as Orual finally discovered when she unveiled, "all of us, with unveiled faces, seeing the glory of the Lord as though reflected in a mirror, are being transformed into the same image from one degree of glory to another; for this comes from the Lord, the Spirit" (2 Cor 3:12–18). Could this be the text that inspired Lewis to add to the myth of Cupid and Psyche by having Orual wear a veil?

The importance of these Biblical passages is that they illuminate the subject of sanctification in a way few theologians have noticed. Paul tells us that instead of an indistinct reflection as from a mirror, we shall one day see "face to face." 1 John 3:2 promises that when we are able to see him as he is, we shall be like him. And in the 2 Corinthians passage just above, Paul tells us that now, though we see the glory of God only as reflected in a mirror, even that is enough to transform us.

Lewis may have been only an "armchair theologian," as he himself would admit, and yet that keen mind fastened on to this truth that many miss. In *Perelandra*, Lewis interrupts the action of the plot to remind us that God's *face* – not just God, but his *face* – is the ultimate destiny of every human. Ransom comes upon Weston, now possessed by Satan, as he is mutilating a number of frog-like creatures. To his horror, Weston looks up at him, and smiles! That smile is so horrible, Ransom faints at the shock, begins to come to, and faints again!

> As he lay there, still unable and perhaps unwilling to rise, it came into his mind that in certain old philosophers and poets he had read that the mere sight of the devils was one of the greatest among the torments of Hell. It had seemed to him till now merely a quaint fancy. And yet (as he now saw) even the children knew better: no child would have any difficulty in understanding that there might be a face the mere beholding of which was final calamity. The children, the poets, and the philosophers were right. As there is one Face above all worlds merely to see which is irrevocable joy, so at the bottom of all worlds that face is waiting whose sight alone is the misery from which none who beholds it can recover. And though there seemed to be, and indeed were, a thousand roads by which a man could walk through the world, there was not a single one which did not lead sooner or later either to the Beatific or Miserific Vision. He himself had, of course, seen only a mask or faint adumbration of it; even so, he was not quite sure that he would live. (PER: 96)

This is why Lewis ended Narnia as he did, with Aslan waiting at the door of the stable. All of Narnia's inhabitants, fleeing the destruction behind them, had no choice but to encounter that divine face. That gets to the heart of the matter. No long lines of billions of people waiting to come before the Judge, no reviews of our entire lives. The judgment will be simple and quick: how we have shaped ourselves by all of our decisions, Lewis reminds us, determines whether that face is a sight of joy or unbearable terror. Either way, the result will be permanent.

> In the end that Face which is the delight or the terror of the universe must be turned upon each of us either with one expression or with the other, either conferring glory inexpressible or inflicting shame that can never be cured or disguised ... It is written that we shall "stand before" Him, shall appear, shall be inspected. The promise of glory is the promise, almost incredible and only possible by the work of Christ, that some of us, that any of us who really chooses, shall actually survive that examination, shall find approval, shall please God. ("Weight of Glory" in WG: 39)

Even now, that face is waiting for each person to unveil. The experience may not be pleasant; having our faults revealed and then put to death is painful. But God's face can be endured, since in this life we see it only indirectly as through a mirror. Will we conceal ourselves like Orual, or choose to live with God like Psyche? "Since that contact cannot be avoided for long, and since it means either bliss or horror, the business of life is to learn to like it" ("Dogma and the Universe" in GID: 47).

Conclusion

The Legacy of Lewis

Did Lewis Pass the Test?

The imagination, wit, and intellect of Lewis have greatly contributed to our understanding of Biblical theology, especially what the future may hold for us and how we should prepare for it now. But every occupation, I suppose, has its dangers and this is certainly true for the theologian. The risk of doing theology is becoming so engrossed in the details that one forgets what theology is all about, and many have succumbed to this risk. I speak as an insider here. Theological books that cause us to marvel at the miracles of Jesus are now increasingly rare. Journal articles that strengthen our resolve to walk by faith and resist all the traps Screwtape has for us are few and far between. Theology has become a cluster of highly specialized and technical fields; a thought-world where scholars explore for a lifetime just one country or even one county of that world.

The dangers of theology may be a strange way to start a conclusion, but Lewis wrote enough about theology for us to regard him as a theologian in his own right. He was quite aware of his unusual gifts and how they could lead to pride. Did Lewis manage to avoid this trap? I believe he did. Standing on the threshold of Heaven, Lewis imagined himself speaking to George MacDonald, his guide in *The Great Divorce*. In a fascinating display of role playing, Lewis uses him to warn himself! After his mentor described someone who was interested only in survival and therefore rejected Heaven because everyone had already survived, Lewis finds this account hard to believe.

"Do ye think so?" said the Teacher with a piercing glance. "It is nearer to such as you than ye think. There have been men before now who got so interested in proving the existence of God that they came to care nothing for God himself...as if the good Lord had nothing to do but *exist!*" The sin Lewis wanted to avoid is the substitution of the means for the end, and, MacDonald warns him, "It is the subtlest of all the snares"(GD: 71).

As I have shown in this study, Lewis kept our Heavenly destination in view. He did not forget that theology is really meant to be a map drawn up by great Christian thinkers before us; a map based on the truths of the Bible that will guide us safely through this world and prepare us for the next, even while "translating" the directions of the map for those who have not learned its language but wish to follow its path.

Another snare has claimed many great thinkers: the error that the map will yield its secrets only to a keen mind. There is much in theology to engage the intellect, but the Source behind the map intended it to be a guide for everyone. In the time of Jesus, the rabbis were also map readers and explainers; interpreting the Law of Moses was often their only occupation. The gospels generally paint a negative picture of them, but in reality, many of them were able to avoid the trap. The entire Law could be fulfilled by loving God and one's neighbor, and Jesus agreed with them (Luke 10:25–28). And when they looked around at humanity and asked who was worthy to inherit the age to come, they generally chose someone like a juggler, who knew nothing about their precious law, but spent his time bringing merriment and encouragement to others.

Like some of the rabbis, and like Paul, who counted everything from his past as rubbish (Phil 3:8), Lewis also realized Heaven did not depend upon his many accomplishments. When he took the test and asked, in effect, "who will be great in the age to come?" his answer was Sarah Smith of Golders Green. Who was she? A nobody on earth. Even the alliteration of her name seems to convey her commonness. Why was she so great in Heaven? And why are there so many people and animals in her train? Because she loved.

> "And who are all these young men and women on each side?"
> "They are her sons and daughters."
> "She must have had a very large family, Sir."
> "Every young man or boy that met her became her son – even if it was only the boy that brought the meat to her back door. Every girl that met her was her daughter."
> "Isn't that a bit hard on their own parents?"
> "No. There *are* those that steal other people's children. But her motherhood was of a different kind. Those on whom it fell went back to their natural parents loving them more. Few men looked on her without becoming, in a certain fashion, her lovers. But it was the kind of love that made them not less true, but truer, to their own wives." (GD: 106)

Yes, she loved. It wasn't education, but love. Not a professorship at Oxford, or fame, or prestige. She probably never went to college or traveled very far from her home. But she became a conduit of God's love to everyone she met. Yes, Lewis passed the test, and we can understand why he became a spiritual mentor for so many. "I most fully allow that it is of more importance for you or me today to refrain from one sneer or to extend one charitable thought to an enemy than to know all that angels and archangels know about the mysteries of the New Creation" (M: 168).

The Impact of Lewis

More than a century after his birth, Lewis has become more popular than ever, though there is a certain irony about the way it has come about. The young man who set out with great determination to become a poet is rarely praised for his poetry today. The Oxford scholar who made significant contributions to the fields of literary criticism and English literature is not a major force in those discussions today. But his career as an "amateur" theologian who set out humbly to explain and defend the Christian faith in his letters, articles, poetry, and books, best accounts for his continuing success today.

That success has taken many forms and reaches into many areas of national life, especially in America. The influence of Lewis is obvious in the writings of many leaders who are involved in politics, in social and cultural causes, and a variety of ministries, including prison reform. Lewis has been influential on fantasy and children's writers, and even the arts. I've personally seen sculptures, song lyrics, and names of music groups that reflect his writings and I'm sure there are many more I haven't seen. Due in large part to *The Chronicles of Narnia*, *The Screwtape Letters*, and *Mere Christianity*, even his lesser-known works remain in print, with new editions regularly appearing. Even George MacDonald has been rescued from obscurity. Thanks to his association with Lewis, his works have been "dusted off" and published in new editions.

And yet, as I have attempted to show, some of the most significant aspects of Lewis's theology are found only in his lesser-known works, such as *Miracles*, *The Problem of Pain*, *Till We Have Faces*, and especially *The Great Divorce*. Symbolism, figurative language, complex discussions, and frequent allusions to and borrowings from a tremendous variety of sources, many from Antiquity, all conspire together to discourage many would-be readers. This study is written with them particularly in mind. I shall have succeeded if the deeper aspects of Lewis's theology are now more accessible, and if the reader is encouraged to pursue a deeper relationship with God. Lewis would have wanted it that way.

A Theology of Redemption

It seems in conclusion that the theology of Lewis is centered around one word: redemption. As a new believer he began to look around at his world and asked: "What on earth (pun intended!) is God up to?" The Scriptures gave him the answer he sought: God has acted and continues to act in human history to restore his world and his universe to himself. That "treatment" includes us, and when our redemption is complete, he will even use us in his redemptive plans for nature, Lewis believed. And after this world . . . the sky is the limit!

God hasn't acted only in our history, but in the spirit world as well. He has prepared a place there for us; an environment designed to continue our sanctification. The understanding of Purgatory is, in my opinion, one of the most important aspects of Lewis's theology. His emphasis upon God's respect for our choices "redeems" the justice of God and removes the stumbling block so many have found in Christianity's insistence that Christ is the only way to God. Everyone has the chance to choose salvation in Christ, and no one will be lost except those who reject Heaven.

Even the story of God becoming man and dying for the world has in a sense a "redemptive" effect for Lewis, for it "redeemed" the ancient myths by showing them as God-given preparations for Christ. And there is another, more personal sense in which God redeems the past; even the pains of the past. The glories of Heaven will "work backward," transforming the meaning of the earthly life of each believer. When we understand how God used our trials and pains to purify us, we will say "I was always in Heaven" (GD: 67–8). Indeed, Lewis believed every life experience can bring us closer to God if we allow him to use them. "God whispers to us in our pleasures, speaks in our conscience, but shouts in our pains; it is His megaphone to rouse a deaf world" (PP: 93).

And Lewis urges his readers to let God redeem the present time. We cannot avoid the face above all worlds, but we can prepare, "down here," by our choices and the grace of God, for the bus ride "up there" to Paradise, and prepare there for that still "higher" revelation of full glory that will bring us into eternity with him, finally sharing his glory and serving him in total freedom.

> Who will trust us with the true wealth if we cannot be trusted even with the wealth that perishes? Who will trust me with a spiritual body if I cannot control even an earthly body? These small and perishable bodies we now have were given to us as ponies are given to schoolboys. We must learn to manage: not that we may some day be free of horses altogether but that some day we may ride bare-back, confident and rejoicing, those greater mounts, those winged, shining and world-shaking horses which perhaps even now expect us with impatience, pawing and snorting in the King's stables. (M: 169)

And they shall see His face. (Rev 22:4)

Bibliography

Adey, Lionel (1998). *C. S. Lewis. Writer, Dreamer and Mentor*. Grand Rapids: Eerdmans.

Downing, David C. (1992). *Planets in Peril. A Critical Study of C. S. Lewis's Ransom Trilogy*. Amherst: University of Massachusetts Press.

Downing, David C. (2002). *The Most Reluctant Convert. C. S. Lewis's Journey to Faith*. Downers Grove, IL: Intervarsity Press.

Ford, Paul F. (1994). *Companion to Narnia*. San Francisco: Harper San Francisco.

Foster, Brett (1998). "An estimation of an admonition: The nature of value, the value of nature, and *The Abolition of Man. Christian Scholar's Review*, XXVII: 4, Summer, pp. 416–35.

Goffar, Janine (1995). *C. S. Lewis Index. Rumours from the Sculptor's Shop*. Riverside, CA: La Sierra University Press.

Hooper, Walter (1996). *C. S. Lewis. A Companion and Guide*. San Francisco: Harper San Francisco.

Hooper, Walter (1998). "The lectures of C. S. Lewis in the universities of Oxford and Cambridge." *Christian Scholar's Review*, XXVII: 4, Summer, pp. 436–53.

Jacobs, Alan (2005). *The Narnian. The Life and Imagination of C. S. Lewis*. San Francisco: Harper San Francisco.

Kreeft, Peter (1994). *C. S. Lewis for the Third Millennium. Six Essays on The Abolition of Man*. San Francisco: Ignatius Press.

Sayers, Dorothy L., J. R. R. Tolkien, C. S. Lewis, etc. (1978). *Essays Presented to Charles Williams*. C. S. Lewis, ed. Grand Rapids: Eerdmans.

Schaeffer, Francis A. (1976). *The God Who is There. Speaking Historic Christianity into the Twentieth Century*. Downers Grove, IL: Intervarsity Press.

Index